Dialogue
with My
Daughters

Dialogue

with My

Daughters

JEFFREY A. JOHNSON, SR.

Dialogue With My Daughters
by Jeffrey A. Johnson, Sr.

Cover Design by Tina Williams, Tru Essence Designs
www.truessencedesign.com

© Copyright 2011

SAINT PAUL PRESS, DALLAS, TEXAS

First Printing, 2011

The Bible quotations used in this volume are from the King James Version, the New International Version, and the New Living Translation.

The name SAINT PAUL PRESS and its logo are registered as a trademark in the U.S. patent office.

ISBN-10: 0-9838328-5-4
ISBN-13: 978-0-9838328-5-0

Printed in the U.S.A.

To all of my spiritual daughters,

I have waited for over two decades to share this dialogue
with you. As you read, I hope and pray you will open
your heart, mind, and soul and be receptive
to my loving, fatherly expressions.
You are the daughters I always wanted to have.

CONTENTS

CHAPTER 1
Handle Your Beliefs
You Are Not Your Hair

CHAPTER 2
Handle Your Body
Keep Your Cookies in the Cookie Jar

CHAPTER 3

Handle Your Brain

Free Your Mind and the Rest Will Follow

CHAPTER 4
Handle Your Business:
Girl, Get Your Money Straight

CHAPTER 5
Handle Your Blessings
Do You

CHAPTER 6
Handle Your Basics
Put a Ring on It

EPILOGUE

FOREWORD

Dr. Frederick D. Haynes, III

A SPORTS HIGHLIGHT that went viral in popularity was really a "lowlight" for one little girl. A father had taken his toddler daughter to a baseball game. He had secured good seats in the front row along the foul line. I'm sure that she was having a wonderful time, not because she was attending a baseball game, but because she was with her daddy. At her age, she spelled "love" like all children spell "love": t-i-m-e. She was sitting on top of the world as she sat in her father's lap, when, all of a sudden, her world was turned upside down. Unbeknownst to this precious female child, a foul ball had been hit in their direction by the baseball player at bat. Her father jumped up to reach for the foul ball and, from the comfort of his lap, ejected her and she tumbled to the ground.

My heart went out to the precious little "princess" because she was dropped by her father due to his prioritized pursuit of something "foul!" Sadly, her experience is a metaphor for the memories of many women, and a painful portrait of girls and young ladies in the present. They know the pain of being dropped, either by a father who went AWOL as they were growing up, or by a daddy who was physically present but emotionally absent. This father-sized void has resulted in wounded women with fractured femininity "looking for love in all the wrong places," trying to fill the void and heal the wound.

Fortunately, Pastor Jeffrey Johnson serves as a shepherd to shattered sisters in this brilliant book. Pastor Johnson powerfully utilizes his exceptional gospel gifts to minister healing and empowering truths that will bless women who had an absentee father and little girls whose father has pulled a disappearing act. Through this tremendous tome, Jeffrey Johnson is serving as a "father to the fatherless."

As much as this wonderful work will bless *women*, speaking as a proud father of a self-professed "daddy's girl," I also greatly benefitted and learned so much from the wealth of wisdom found in these pages. All fathers should read this book. Every man who has to interact with women will find eye-opening insights that will inform their behavior with those of the fairer sex.

As you read this book you, like me, will thank God for the healing truths that will bless a generation broken by dysfunctional families, and set the stage for: families to be functional, relationships to be repaired, women to check themselves so they won't wreck themselves, and men to step up and man up! In this book, women who've been "dropped" will be picked up.

Thank God for Pastor Jeffrey Johnson and this book that promises to be a "game-changer!"

Dr. Frederick D. Haynes, III
Senior Pastor
Friendship-West Baptist Church
Dallas, Texas

INTRODUCTION

Jeffrey A. Johnson, Sr.

ONE SUNDAY AFTER CHURCH, a young woman came up to me and said, "Pastor, I just want to thank you for talking to us about things like a father. I have never had a daddy in my life, and I know that's true for other girls here at the church. Thank you for filling that gap in our lives." Her words found a special place in my heart.

Four times, I have been in the labor and delivery room with my wife: February 20, 1988; June 16, 1990; July 11, 1993; and August 23, 1997. Each time we went into that room, we had no idea if we were having a boy or a girl. We didn't want to know the gender in advance. We entered the room each time with great joy and anticipation, not knowing what God was giving us. It would stand to reason, though, that at least one out of four babies would be a girl.

The first time, the doctor said, "Congratulations! Ten pounds and one ounce. It's a boy!" The next time, he announced, "Congratulations! Eight pounds and two ounces. It's a boy!" The third time, we thought sure it was going to be a girl. "Congratulations!" we heard. "Eight pounds and three ounces. It's a boy!" Then the last time, I said to myself, "This is it. This time it's a girl. I know God is going to give me my daughter this time." "Congratulations!" the doctor said. "Four pounds, five ounces. It's a boy!"

Now, let me be clear. I did not ever have a sense of disappointment at the birth of any of my children. I was excited and happy with the birth of each of my sons. Each one of them is special, and I love them from the depths of my heart. It's just that, from the time we began envisioning our family, we always imagined having a daughter among our children.

For more than twenty years, we have had her name picked out. There were so many things we wanted to pass along to her—life lessons, spiritual truths, parental advice, and lots and lots of love. I already knew how I would raise her, how I would nurture her, and how we would spend time together. I knew how I would talk with her, care for her, and encourage her as she grew. I knew we were going to have wonderful times together. I recognized that it would be my responsibility to communicate certain things to her, so I had already envisioned the kind of dialogues we would have. But, I have come to the realization and acceptance that I am not going to have a daughter; it just isn't going to happen.

Along with that realization came a revelation from God. One day, He spoke to my spirit, saying, "Jeffrey Johnson, I did not give you a biological daughter, but I have given you plenty of spiritual daughters." There are thousands of girls and young women within my church and the churches around the country where I am invited to preach. *They* are my spiritual daughters, the objects of my fatherly love and compassion. So, as I have prepared my sermons over the years, I have had my daughters in mind, along with others to whom God has wanted to speak.

Now God has given me the desire to put into print some of the talks I would have had with my own daughter, had God blessed me in that way. I offer them now instead to the young women, (and the not so young), who have not had a father to reach out and talk with them about some of these critical matters. There are some women, too, who have had fathers, but for whatever reasons, those men were not able to have father-daughter talks with them. And I believe that even those who have been fortunate enough to have had conversations with their fathers can still benefit from hearing these things again. Going yet one step further, I believe that fathers who read this book can learn how to approach their own daughters so they can have the kind of talks that are so crucial for their relationships.

I entitled this book *A Dialogue with My Daughters* because I want you to interact with what you are reading. A *dialogue* takes place between two people; it isn't just one person doing all the talking. I don't want you to simply read something and then move on. I want you to take time to reflect upon it; think about how it is meaningful to you; remember situations in which it is applicable; and then ask what God is saying to you through this. To better enable you to do this, I have also written *A Dialogue with My Daughters: My Personal Reflections*, an accompanying journal that you can use for that interaction process. This book is intended to change your life, not just to fill your mind with information. That will only happen if you make the time to process what you are reading and interact with what I am saying as we go along.

For all of my spiritual daughters, please understand that what you are reading is coming from my heart, and from God's heart. I love you very much, and know that God has some special things that He wants to do with you and in you. Let me share with you what we will be discussing in this book.

Chapter 1: *Handle Your Beliefs: You Are Not Your Hair* (Psalm 139:13-18)

Daughter, in order to live out your full potential and become the woman God wants you to be, you must recognize that you are a spiritual being, made in the image of God. You are more than your hair and skin. You are soul, mind, emotion, and will. You have been created for the pleasure of God. To fulfill your greatness:

You must believe in God.

You must believe God.

You must believe what God says about you.

You are fearfully and wonderfully made.

Chapter 2: *Handle Your Body: Keep Your Cookies in the Cookie Jar* (1 Corinthians 6:12-20)

I want to remind you that ultimately you were created by the Lord for the Lord. God made your body just the way He wanted it. You should accept and appreciate it.

Accept and appreciate that your body is the Lord's.

Accept and appreciate that your body is the temple of
God.

Accept and appreciate that the Spirit of God lives in you. Because of this, you should avoid sexual immorality and keep your cookies in the cookie jar until the appropriate time.

Chapter 3: *Handle Your Brain: Free Your Mind and the Rest Will Follow* (Romans 12:2)

Daughter, be not conformed to this world. This world has a pattern for perversion. This world has a pattern for distorted friendships, relationships, family, dress, money management and communication. This world operates outside the will of God.

You must transform your mind.

You must think differently from this world.

You must change your mind to agree with God.

Your mentality will determine your destiny. Your choices will determine your consequences. The path God chooses for you should be the path you choose for yourself.

Chapter 4: *Handle Your Business: Girl, Get Your Money Straight* (Proverbs 31)

Daughter, you are so special in my eyes and in the sight of God. Do not spend your life waiting for a man to do for you what you can do for yourself. You do not need a man for affirmation, confirmation or identification; you already have that in God.

> You will prosper when you are a producer, not merely a consumer.
>
> You will prosper when you plan your purchases, rather than being an impulse shopper.
>
> You will prosper when you plant seeds by giving to the poor.
>
> You will prosper when you overcome psychological barriers that hold you back.
>
> You will prosper when you praise God.

Do not waste time and energy trying to straighten out a man. Instead, focus on getting your money straight.

Chapter 5: *Handle Your Blessings: Do You* (1 Kings 10)

Daughter, the queen of Sheba was a very blessed sister. She was blessed with royalty, riches and self-respect. She knew how to handle her blessings. She didn't pretend to be any less than she was in order to be more attractive to a man. Nor did she try to be someone else.

> She teaches you to be analytical, not just emotional; she
> asked hard questions.
> She teaches you not to be easily impressed.
> She teaches you to be sensible.

Just as the queen of Sheba returned to her own place, be sure you find your place in Christ and learn to handle your blessings.

Chapter 6 Handle Your Basics: Put a Ring on It (Matthew 25:1-13)

Daughter, when the day comes that you are serious about a man, be sure that he is willing to put a ring on your finger and commit his life to you. Make sure that you also are ready for the highest level of commitment. Be mindful that: readiness precedes weddings; patience precedes prenuptials; and spirituality precedes matrimony. When you enter the door of marriage, which leads you to a new life with the one you love, recognize that you are leaving all other men behind, on the other side of that door. You know that I love you; therefore, I am not willing to give you to just any man. Some of the things I will look for before giving my blessing include:

> He must be a fully committed Christian and demonstrate
> Christlike character.
> He must work and be responsible.
> He must have demonstrated genuine love and affection
> towards you.

After these things are apparent, and your wedding day arrives, the question will be asked: "Who gives this woman to be married to this man?" With overwhelming joy, I will respond, "I do."

CHAPTER 1

Handle Your Beliefs

You Are Not Your Hair

For you created my inmost being;
    you knit me together in my mother's womb.
I praise you because I am fearfully and wonderfully made;
    your works are wonderful,
    I know that full well.
My frame was not hidden from you
    when I was made in the secret place,
    when I was woven together in the depths of the earth.
Your eyes saw my unformed body;
    all the days ordained for me were written
        in your book
    before one of them came to be.
How precious to me are your thoughts, God!
How vast is the sum of them!
Were I to count them,
    they would outnumber the grains of sand—
    when I awake, I am still with you.

PSALM 139:13-18

A FAIRY TALE

Daughter, let me tell you a fairy tale. Listen very carefully. There was a young woman who stood in front of her mirror every morning. She looked into that mirror and asked, "Mirror, mirror, on the wall, who's the finest one of all?" The mirror would always reply, "You are the finest one of all." This went on day after day, week after week, month after month, and year after year. Her daily ritual was always the same. She would ask, "Mirror, mirror, on the wall, who's the finest one of all?" And, the mirror would tell her, "You are the finest one of all." Then one day she asked that mirror, "Who's the finest one of them all?" And, the mirror responded, "It's not you." The mirror continued, "It's another girl. She's got longer hair. Her hair is blond. She has got fairer skin. She's younger than you and in better shape. She's the finest one of all."

When the mirror said that, the young woman became envious, and developed into a hater. She went on Facebook and lied about this other girl, saying she was playing around with seven different boyfriends. She said and did everything she could to destroy this girl's reputation, all because she believed that girl was finer than she was. But that girl didn't have seven boyfriends, and she wasn't playing around with anybody. She didn't want just anybody. She wanted a prince and was living her life in such a way that a prince would be attracted to her. But the young woman whose mirror had betrayed her tried to make this beautiful girl appear ugly in the sight of others.

Daughter, the moral of the story is this: mirrors don't talk. The mirror was simply a reflection of the young woman's projections. She projected onto the mirror what she thought of herself. When she thought of herself as fine, her mirror "told her" she was fine. But when she saw another girl who seemed to have some qualities that she thought were better than hers, her mirror "told her" that she was no longer so fine and the other girl looked better than she did. The mirror was just a reflection of her own mindset.

OUR BELIEFS DETERMINE OUR BEHAVIOR

This story also teaches that whatever we believe dictates how we behave. When the young woman believed that she was fine, she treated others well. She was not envious or jealous of others because she felt okay about herself. But when she believed that she wasn't as good as someone else, she behaved badly toward that other person. In order to try to regain her positive image of herself, she tried to put down the other person and to diminish her in the eyes of others. She thought that if she could make the other girl look bad, she would look better herself. Yet the fact is that her beauty had not lessened at all. She was still fine. It was only her image of herself that had changed. But what she now believed about herself dictated the way she behaved.

One of the problems this young woman had from the start is that she didn't know how to define beauty. You see, baby girl, there is no one universal definition for beauty. Beauty varies from person to person, from country to country, and from culture to culture. What isn't necessarily attractive to one person is beautiful to somebody else. As the old saying goes, "Beauty is in the eye of the beholder." That's why how you view yourself is so important. Whatever you think about yourself internally is what you will see when you look in the mirror externally.

When you look in the mirror, what do you see? "Real Girls, Real Pressure: A National Report on the State of Self-Esteem," compiled in 2008 by the Dove Self-Esteem Fund, revealed some upsetting statistics: the majority of girls (71 percent), believe they are not good enough or do not measure up in their looks, school performance, and relationships with family and friends; a girl's self-esteem is based more on how she *views* her own body weight and shape than how much she actually weighs; 75 percent of girls with low self-esteem engage in ways that are hurtful to themselves (e.g., eating disorders, smoking, drinking, cutting, etc.); and 61 percent talk negatively about themselves.

Self-loathing, depression, and unhealthy eating habits, along with so many other negative behaviors, stem from a poor self-image. Sadly, we live in a country that is obsessed with weight. A 2006 University of Minnesota "Project Eat" study revealed that 62 percent of teen girls used "unhealthy weight control habits," and 21.9 percent actually resorted to diet pills, laxatives, vomiting, or skipping meals to lose weight. A Student Wellness website posted by the University of Colorado at Boulder states that in 1990, the average age of a girl who started dieting was eight, as opposed to the average age of fourteen in 1970. That same website reports, "Young girls are more afraid of becoming fat than they are of nuclear war, cancer, or losing their parents." Part of the problem, as the website infers, comes from the "ideal" images that confront females everywhere: "The 'ideal' woman—portrayed by models, Miss America, Barbie dolls, and screen actresses—is 5'5, weighs 100 pounds and wears a size 5."

HEALTHY CHOICES MAKE A HEALTHY BODY

We are so obsessed with weight that when we are simply doing what is healthy for us, people assume that we are dieting. During a time that I was training to run a marathon, I ordered a vegetable plate while having lunch with a friend. This friend knew that because I was training to run a marathon, I was running thirty or forty miles a week and eating right, but he still asked, "How much weight are you trying to lose?" I said, "I'm not trying to lose any weight." But getting to our natural body weight will be a by-product of eating right, exercising regularly, and getting enough sleep.

If I eat right (without lying to myself that "just a few" French fries, milkshakes, and chocolate brownies are good for me), and exercise right (without fooling myself into believing that clicking the remote constitutes exercise), I don't have to be concerned with how much I weigh. If I am honestly and faithfully doing what is right for my body, I do not need to diet or worry about what I see on the scales. Unless there is some medical reason that I am carrying too much weight (which would prompt an immediate trip to the doctor), I can trust God that being faithful in caring for His temple will bring me to that weight I am intended to be.

Now, what is a healthy weight for me may be overweight or underweight for someone else of my height. We don't all have the same body types. While one 5'4" woman with a small frame may be healthy at 120 pounds, a woman of the same height with a large frame may be healthy at 145 pounds. We can't do much to change our genetic propensity, so we shouldn't try to make ourselves fit another's image. You cannot compare yourself to somebody else in order to determine how beautiful you are.

WHO DEFINES "BEAUTY" FOR YOU?

We live in a sex-crazed culture that has influenced and shaped our mentality. Through magazines, movies, videos, songs, and all sorts of advertising, our culture tries to tell us what's beautiful. In this world, beauty is most often defined by what is sexy and seductive. So, instead of looking to the Bible as our barometer for beauty, we look to the world. We try to emulate what we see celebrities doing and wearing. Rather than looking beautiful in God's sight, a woman may only care how she looks to some man who doesn't even care about her relationship with God. He may tell her that she looks beautiful when she is wearing short skirts and low-cut tops, even though God's Word tells her to dress modestly.

Young girls are piercing their eyebrows, lips, noses, tongues, and even their navels and nipples because someone in this sex-crazed society has told them that is beautiful. Or, they may have heard a subliminal message: "You can't be beautiful, but at least you can be different." So, a girl whose mirror tells her she's not attractive resorts to piercings or tattoos to find some way of garnering attention. She thinks that if she cannot fit into the world of those who are beautiful, at least she can fit into a group that will look at the decoration of her body and say, "Cool!" Sadly, she doesn't realize most of the others in that group are influenced by the same negative self-image she has.

Daughter, please be sure that you look to God to find out how beautiful you are. Feel confident from His Word that you are fearfully and wonderfully made. If you allow other people to define you, then they can confine you. If you allow other people to label you, then they can limit you. As I am talking to you right now, I recognize and honor the fact that you are old enough to make your own decisions. You can read God's Word for yourself. You can hear the Holy Spirit speaking to you for yourself. You don't need your daddy to tell you what is right and wrong anymore. So often, it isn't even a question about whether or not something is right or wrong, anyhow. The question is: why are you doing it? The question is not whether it is right or wrong to pierce your nipple, your navel, or your private parts. The question is: why do you feel you need to pierce it?

For some young women, the reason is an unmet need for their daddy's attention. Focus on the Family founder Dr. James Dobson points out that because their daddy wasn't present in their lives, it has left a void inside of them. They wanted that attention, but never got it. Now they have come to the realization that they are never going to get that attention from their father. Subconsciously, they think, "Daddy, I wanted you to like me. I would have done anything to make you like me. But you aren't even here, so I'll just find someone else who will like me." They look for that attention, affection, and affirmation from a boyfriend, from a man. If this man doesn't like them the way that God made them, they will change the way they were made so that the man will like them, even as they would have "done anything" to get their daddy to like them.

Without accepting the fact that they are wonderfully made by God, young women are vulnerable to the opinions of others. If a young woman knows she is fine, and has seen that fine image in her mirror before she left the house, she is going to adorn herself and carry herself as a woman of beauty and value. She is going to be *showing* others how beautiful she is, not *asking* others how beautiful she is. It's about perception. If she has a positive self-image, she doesn't need for someone else to give her a reason to value herself. If, however, she has a negative self-image, she will constantly look for someone who will offer her attention and affirmation—even if it comes as a result of engaging in some negative behavior in her life.

IMPEDED BY PERCEPTION

As T.D. Jakes says, "It's perception." The way our perceptions are typically formed is through believing what others have told us. Most women who know they are fine have had someone tell them that. They've heard it often enough, in fact, that their self-perception is that they are fine. The opposite is also true. Women who believe they are not attractive and who see only what they consider to be flaws in their appearance have had someone telling them they are not attractive, and someone pointing out what that person considered to be flaws. These women now hold the perception that they are unattractive and they cannot imagine anyone thinking otherwise about them. Their own mentality is holding them back.

I'm an *American Idol* fan for about the first two weeks of each new season. I don't watch to find out who will be the ultimate champion. I watch it for the comedy value. I like to see people who can't sing any better than I can, (and I can't sing), stand in front of millions of people and bellow out a tune. I don't understand why they would do that, but I find it funny to watch.

One night, *American Idol* had gone to Milwaukee, and hundreds of people were auditioning to try to get on the show. A young woman in her early twenties began singing in front of the three judges, but they stopped her before she could finish. They were getting ready to explain to her what she needed to do to better her performance, but before they could say anything, she started talking. She said, "Y'all didn't vote for me because y'all think I'm big." Randy Jackson, one of the judges, countered her argument by pointing out another contestant and saying, "We just voted him on, and he's twice the size you are. So it isn't because you're too big." Still not willing to listen, she reacted, "Well, he's a man. And, I can out-sing more than half of these people, and y'all didn't vote for me 'cause I'm too big, and that's the problem with this!" Then she ran off the stage. Randy Jackson commented, "We didn't even have to vote her off. She voted herself off."

This young woman could not receive advice from those who wanted to help her improve her performance because she has a warped perception of herself. She thinks she is too big, and now she thinks everyone else is seeing her through her own mirror. She thinks everybody else sees her as being too big. Her perception is working against her. Even when others are trying to point her in the right direction, she can't believe that they could see anything good in her, anything worth cultivating. Instead, before even listening to what they had to say, she concluded that they stopped her because she is too big, so she voted herself off.

Daughter, I don't want you to vote yourself off. When you go for that degree, I don't want you to make up your mind in advance that you can't get it. When you attempt to start your own company, I don't want you to vote yourself off, saying, "Who do I think I am? I can never own my own company." I don't want you to vote yourself off from a healthy relationship. When that good man approaches you with interest, I don't want you to say, "This can't work. When he really gets to know me, he won't like me. It will be easier to stop it now before he can hurt me." Baby girl, don't vote yourself off. You are a winner. You *can* accomplish your goals. You *are* of value. You *are* fine.

More than Skin Deep

Part of the problem we have in our society regarding appearance is that we have misdefined beauty. Too often, we have been brainwashed about what it means to be beautiful. For years, we have let the wrong people define beauty for us. Some have told us that we can buy it at a cosmetic counter. Some have offered it through plastic surgery and surgical implants. Some have said that it can be enhanced by Botox injections. Some have promised that it comes with this or that product. Some say a certain garment will bring it. How greatly we need to redefine beauty!

Beauty isn't based on being from a particular country or culture. It can't be tattooed or pierced on. It can't be surgically implanted. It can't be bought in a cosmetic tube; in fact, beauty cannot be bought at all. A man doesn't make you beautiful when he comes into your life, and, if a relationship doesn't work, he doesn't take your beauty away when he leaves. We have to redefine beauty. We need to ask God for His definition.

First Samuel 16:7 says, "People look at the outward appearance, but the LORD looks at the heart." We've got to start defining beauty from God's perspective. Since beauty differs from person to person, country to country, and culture to culture, we need to find a definition that works for all of us. Beauty isn't only about the appearance on the outside, but also what is residing on the inside. The first time a man ever looked upon a woman, Adam said of Eve, in Genesis 2:23, "This is now bone of my bones and flesh of my flesh . . . ." The man first acknowledged the bone, and then the flesh. He first acknowledged what was on the inside that couldn't be seen before mentioning what was visible on the outside. Adam was a man into whom God had breathed His own life, a man who enjoyed an awesome personal relationship with God. When this man looked upon the woman God had made, he saw her from the inside out, not from the outside in.

My daughter, find a man who is looking first at who you are on the inside. If a man is only concerned with what you look like on the outside, God has not yet breathed life into him, and you will be living with death if you enter into a relationship with that person. A man worth having will recognize your inner beauty, as stated in 1 Peter 3:3-4: "Your beauty should not come from outward adornment, such as elaborate hairstyles and the wearing of gold jewelry or fine clothes. Rather, it should be that of your inner self, the unfading beauty of a gentle and quiet spirit, which is of great worth in God's sight." This doesn't mean that you are not to get your hair done, put on makeup, or wear nice clothes or fine jewelry. It means that your beauty and your concept of beauty have got to be more than that. It has to go beyond your hair. It's got to be internal.

As you've undoubtedly recognized, I've borrowed the title of this chapter from India Arie, who sings, "I am not my hair; I am not this skin. I am a soul that lives within." She points out that we're confused about who we are. She says we run around thinking that good hair means wearing it a certain way, but it isn't the way we wear our hair that defines who we are; it's the person on the inside.

THE WAY GOD SEES YOU

We've got to redefine what beauty is all about. If we are made in the image of God and in such a way that God Himself knows us intimately, loves us unconditionally, and wants to be with us eternally, how can we dare think that we are anything less than beautiful? Psalm 139:1 says that God has searched us and known us. He knows when we get up and when we sit down. He knows when we move and when we sit still. God knows us so well that it's too awesome to even comprehend. Let me ask you a question: If God valued us enough to send His Son Jesus to earth to die for us, doesn't that mean there is something about us that He finds of great worth? How can we listen to what some mere mortal has to say about us, rather than listen to the One who paid such a huge price to have a relationship with us?

Determine even now that if there is ever some boy or man who has something negative to say about you, you will weigh that against what God has to say about you. This is GOD we're talking about. On one hand, you have a finite creature who probably doesn't even know beauty when he sees it, and who certainly doesn't know you; and on the other hand, you have the Creator of the universe; the One who died for you; the One who knows you intimately and loves you fully; the One who provides for your every need; the One who has been with you always and has promised never to leave you nor forsake you. Whose opinion are you going to receive? Psalm 139:7-10 (KJV) says that God is always with you: "Whither shall I go from thy spirit? or whither shall I flee from thy presence? If I ascend up into heaven, thou art there: if I make my bed in hell, behold, thou art there. If I take the wings of the morning, and dwell in the uttermost parts of the sea; Even there shall thy hand lead me, and thy right hand shall hold me." There is no place you can go that God's presence will not be with you. And God is with you even though He knows everything about you. There are some folk who are with us only because they don't know us. God knows every negative thought we've ever had, every sin we've ever committed, and every unkind thing we have ever said, yet still He is with us.

Human beings are fickle. Some folk will only be with you when you are low down; when you haven't got anything; when you are lower than they are. But, if you ascend into high places— if you get that bachelor's degree, that master's degree, that doctorate, that promotion—they will abandon you because they don't want to be with anyone who has gone any higher than they have. They will walk out on you when your success makes them uncomfortable. They will leave you when you start making choices that take you in an opposite direction from the direction they are choosing. If they can't drag you down with them, they will turn away from you. But God isn't going to abandon you. He is still with you—no matter what.

THE CONSTANCY OF GOD

But, you may wonder, what about those who become low down? Sure, God will be with those who go up into the heavens, but what about those who spiral downward instead? Will God still be with them? Verse 8 says, "If I make my bed in hell, behold, thou art there." Yes, God will be with us even when we descend from the heavenly places—from the place of success and accomplishment in serving God— into hellish places. Fornication can lead us to a hellish place of sexually transmitted diseases, unwanted pregnancies, and messed-up relationships. Adultery (sleeping with someone else's spouse, or someone other than our own spouse) also places us in a hell of our own making.

Whenever we choose to disobey God's Word and engage in activities that dishonor Him, we are making our bed in a hellish place. But even then, God is with us. Even though it is our own fault we are there and we have no one to blame but ourselves, God is not going to leave us. God has enough mercy, enough grace, and enough love that He won't leave us. But neither does He allow us to be content to stay in a hellish place. He transforms us into His likeness and puts a new heart within us that desires things that are above. God takes us by the hand, brings us out of the hellish places, and helps us to find a new place to rest.

God Handles Our Monsters

Daughter, because I want to be a good father, I called friends of mine who have daughters and asked them what they taught their daughters and what I should teach you. Dr. Theron Williams said that when his daughter was a little girl, she came running into her parents' room one night and jumped in bed with him and her mother because she was afraid. She told them that there were monsters under her bed. Now, as much as they love their daughter, they were not going to let her sleep in their bed with them. When Dr. Williams told her she couldn't stay there, she said, "But, Daddy, there are monsters under my bed." "Okay, baby. Come on, let's go," he responded, as he took her by the hand and led her back into her bedroom. "Show me the monsters," he told her.

"Daddy, they are under the bed."

"Baby, I don't see any monsters under the bed."

"Daddy, they are there."

"Okay, come on. Get into bed."

He put her in bed and then sat on the bed with her. Suddenly his little girl started smiling and was happy. Trying to understand her change of demeanor, he asked, "Are there still monsters under your bed?"

"Yes."

"Then how come you aren't afraid anymore? Why are you smiling now and not scared?"

"'Cause, Daddy, you're in the bed with me."

Dr. Williams uses that illustration to let us know that God can handle monsters under the bed. And God can also handle monsters *in* the bed. Daughter, I know that this world can be a frightening place. Sometimes, even when you can't see them, you know that monsters are lurking around. Just be sure that you always take your heavenly Father into your bed with you. His presence will keep the monsters away. He will also give you discernment to distinguish the monster from the man of purpose who loves God, who loves you, and who is worthy of sharing your life, and your bed, with you.

God's presence will also protect you, baby—sometimes by preserving what you already have, but other times by taking away what you have. You have to understand that God loves you so much that He isn't going to let some monster disguised in a Prince Charming costume attack you, harm you, and threaten even worse. God will take that monster out of your life. Sometimes, though, women get so lonely that after God rescues them from such a monster, they keep trying to get him back. They go after what God says they shouldn't have. Sometimes, God's blessing comes from what He takes *from* you, not only what He gives *to* you. If God frees you from a monster, stay free! Don't go back to something that you know is wrong. God is trying to protect you.

NO DOGS ALLOWED

Always remember, baby girl, that you are fearfully and wonderfully made. When you know that God made you and you are His daughter, you are not fooled by finances; you're not tricked by trinkets; you're not manipulated by money; you are not coerced by cash; and you are not misled by lies. The girls and women who don't know that are the ones who end up in unhealthy relationships.

Even when a good man comes along, they vote themselves

out of the relationship immediately. They see a man who is filled with the Spirit of God, loves God, gives to God, and lives for God. But when he shows an interest in them, they sever the relationship even before it gets started. They do that because they don't know that they are fearfully and wonderfully made. They think, "I'm not good enough to have a man like this," so they prevent a relationship from happening. But when a thug comes up who isn't about anything, they are willing to allow a relationship to grow. Even though it is likely subconscious, they think, "This is all I deserve. I don't deserve any better than this."

They may think, too, that our society is such a culture of dogs that they will never meet anyone except a dog. It's not hard to understand why they would feel that way. We seem to love dogs. We greet each other with, "What's up, dog?" Snoop Dogg writes, "Snoop D.O. Double G!" Even Elvis Presley got in on it in his day: "Ain't nothin' but a hound dog . . . ." From Anselm Douglas and the Baha Men, we've got: "Who let the dogs out? Woof, woof, woof, woof!" We love dogs. Even "Atomic Dog!" But Jesus would remind us that dogs are meant to be pets, not partners. He counseled us in Matthew 7:6 not to give that which is holy to dogs.

I wish you and other women could hear some of the brothers in the locker room. I was active in sports as I was growing up, and I know what they say. Actually, they think you're fine. They think you're beautiful. They know you're valuable, but they aren't going to tell you that because they want to mess with your mentality. They know that the less you think of yourself, the more they can do with you. Don't find yourself among those women who are giving themselves to dogs.

FROM FINE TO REFINED

Now that you have learned to redefine beauty, I want you also to learn to *refine* it. Begin every morning when you get up. Look in the mirror and say, "Mirror, mirror, on the wall, who's the finest one of all?" And then say confidently, "I am! I'm fine! I'm beautiful! I'm fearfully made! I'm wonderfully made! I'm a marvelous work of God!" Keep telling yourself that until you believe it! It is the truth. You are fine. You were born fine. Now you just need to refine what you were born with. You were born beautiful; now it's time to refine that.

You were born a beautiful original. When God made you, He didn't make anyone else just like you. As anybody will tell you, an original is worth more than any copy. The problem, however, is that even though you have been born a valuable original, you must be careful not to die a cheap copy, trying to look like somebody else, talk like somebody else, and act like somebody else. There is nothing wrong with you just as you are.

God did not make you too tall, too short, too wide, or too thin. God didn't make you too thick, too skinny, too dark, too light, too black, or too white. God made you just the way He wanted you to be. Revelation 4:11 tells us that God has created everything for His pleasure. You need only to refine your beauty. If you know you're fine, then dress as if you're fine. Comb your hair as if you're fine. Walk as if you're fine. Talk as if you're fine. Demand respect as if you're fine. That's refining your beauty.

In Song of Solomon 1:5, we hear an African woman saying, "I'm black and beautiful" because she knows she's fine. But in the very next verse, she says, "Don't look at me. I've been burned because I've been exposed to the sun. My brothers were angry with me and had me work their fields while neglecting my own."

Notice that she starts by saying she is black and beautiful, but she doesn't refine it. Instead, she then says that she is not what she used to be because she got burned by being in nonreciprocal relationships in which she was doing all the work, but the men were doing nothing for her.

Nonreciprocal relationships will take away from you what God has given to you. You must avoid any relationship in which you are the only one loving, the only one supporting, and the only one giving because you are going to get burned. Rather, you've got to refine what God has given you.

POLISH YOURSELF FOR GOD

Let me illustrate what I mean. When my sons came home from college one summer, they asked if they could use one of my cars. I responded, "Yes, you can use it. Just be careful, and come back at a decent hour. Respect your mama, and don't be coming back here at all times of the night." They said okay. They used the car, they were careful, and they came back at the right time. But they brought the car back dirty and empty. I asked them, "Sons, why is it when you borrowed my car, knowing it's mine, that you brought it back in worse condition than when I gave it to you? I gave it to you clean and filled with gas. You brought it back dirty and empty."

I continued, "Sons, I once had to borrow your grandmother's car. Your grandmother drove a light blue Mercedes. I had to borrow it because my car was in the shop. But before I gave it back to her, I had it washed, detailed, and filled with gas. I didn't give back to her any less than what she gave to me. I gave it back better than when she gave it to me."

Daughter, God has blessed you with beauty. Someday you are going to meet your Savior and Creator and give yourself back to Him. When you do so, be sure you give yourself to Him clean and filled with the Holy Spirit. Don't hang out in places that will make you dirty, or do things that will make you dirty. Don't connect with brothers who take too much out of you. When you give yourself back to God, make sure you are clean and filled. Even now, if you confess your sins, God is faithful and just to forgive you of your sins and cleanse you from all unrighteousness (1 John 1:9). If you are empty right now, God will fill you with His Holy Spirit. Just ask Him. He will not withhold from you any good thing.

Baby girl, you are more than just skin and hair and outward appearance. Let God help you to refine the inner you. The One who made you can remake you. He can cleanse you and fill you. He can teach you how to be the beautiful person He created you to be. Get your beauty advice from the Bible, not from a magazine. Get your beauty treatments from God, not from the cosmetic counter. Adorn yourself with the garment of praise, not simply the latest styles. Live like a princess waiting for her prince to come along, not like a dogcatcher waiting for a stray dog to walk by. Call on your heavenly Father whenever you are afraid or uncertain. Know that He is at your side, where He will protect you, guide you, and give you love that is intimate, gracious, and never failing. As much as I love you, He loves you even more.

CHAPTER 2

Handle Your Body

Keep Your Cookies in the Cookie Jar

You say, "I am allowed to do anything"—but not everything is good for you. And even though "I am allowed to do anything," I must not become a slave to anything. You say, "Food was made for the stomach, and the stomach for food." (This is true, though someday God will do away with both of them.) But you can't say that our bodies were made for sexual immorality. They were made for the Lord, and the Lord cares about our bodies. And God will raise us from the dead by his power, just as he raised our Lord from the dead. Don't you realize that your bodies are actually parts of Christ? Should a man take his body, which is part of Christ, and join it to a prostitute? Never! And don't you realize that if a man joins himself to a prostitute, he becomes one body with her? For the Scriptures say, "The two are united into one." But the person who is joined to the Lord is one spirit with him. Run from sexual sin! No other sin so clearly affects the body as this one does. For sexual immorality is a sin against your own body. Don't you realize that your body is the temple of the Holy Spirit, who lives in you and was given to you by God? You do not belong to yourself, for God bought you with a high price. So you must honor God with your body.

1 CORINTHIANS 6:12-20, NLT

A DIFFERENT KIND OF COOKIE MONSTER

In the 1960s, television producer Joan Ganz Cooney got an idea for using national television to improve the literacy of children in America. She developed a show that focused on teaching preschoolers fundamental reading and math skills. She called the show *Sesame Street. Sesame Street* became very popular, very successful, and very helpful in teaching reading, counting and math skills. Big Bird, Oscar and other regular characters appeared alongside special guests: actors and entertainers who helped teach the children.

Cookie Monster was one of the characters on the show. He acted as if he had some sense—until he saw a cookie. Then he became a different person. He lost sight of everything else as he pursued his goal, yelling, "Cookie! Cookie! Me want cookie!" He lost his focus. He didn't care about what the children at home were learning. He didn't care about the guest stars. He temporarily lost his mind and became disrespectful, knocking things over, treating people badly, and ignoring the lesson being taught to the children. He no longer cared about anything but getting that cookie.

Daughter, every now and then, you are going to run into some boy, some young man, or some grown man who just can't focus. The only thing he thinks about is cookies. He doesn't care about your mind, your learning, or your future. He doesn't care about your hopes, your dreams, your thoughts, your feelings, or your emotions. The only thing he wants from you is your cookies. My counsel to you is that when you run into this person, keep your cookies in the cookie jar. There is an appropriate time, an appropriate place, and an appropriate person designed just for you. Until the time that you come together in marriage, handle your body and keep your cookies in the cookie jar.

NOT AFRAID, BUT ALERT

We live in a time in which this culture is sexually sick. Something is wrong with us. We are sex crazed and sex hyped.

We engage in cybersex and sexting instead of texting. Sexual predators are devouring women and even little girls. Referencing the U.S. Department of Justice 2007 *National Crime Victimization Survey*, RAINN (Rape, Abuse, and Incest National Network) reports that in the United States, someone is sexually assaulted every two minutes. They also state that, of the victims, 80 percent are under the age of thirty, and 44 percent are under the age of eighteen. In an article about dating violence against adolescent girls, in the August 1, 2001 issue of the *Journal of the American Medical Association*, Dr. Jay G. Silverman and his associates found in 1997 and 1999 surveys of ninth- through twelfth-grade female students that one in five "reported being physically and/or sexually abused by a dating partner."

I don't tell you this, Daughter, to make you afraid, but simply to make you aware. A lot of innocent girls have been victims of sexual abuse because they weren't aware that someone who was supposed to care about them could instead mistreat them. You don't need to be afraid of men, but you do need to be alert to anything a man says or does that makes you feel uncomfortable. When that happens, you must immediately get out of that situation.

Some men have allowed their minds to become so perverted that they don't think as healthy men think. They have gotten caught up in "sextracurricular" activities. In an August 22, 2005, website article entitled "Pornified America—The Culture of Pornography," Dr. R. Albert Mohler Jr. wrote, "According to industry studies, seventy percent of eighteen-to-twenty-four-year-old men visit pornographic sites in a typical month."

In its online "Facts about Pornography," the Concerned Women for America reports, "There are 4.2 million pornographic websites (12 percent of total websites)," and "40 million adults in the U.S. regularly visit Internet pornography websites." Those same figures are found on numerous websites. A few sources report even as many as 370 million pornographic websites on the Internet. It seems that such statistics are hard to determine, but it is clear that pornography on the Internet is a multibillion dollar industry and it is attracting millions of regular visitors who are developing warped ideas about sex and warped attitudes toward women. As a people, we have become sick sexually. We need sexual healing.

God didn't create your body for sexual immorality, or "fornication" (KJV). The Greek word used in this context is *pornia*, from which we get our word "pornography." God says that he did not create your body for *pornia*—for pornography, fornication, adultery, or any type of sexual immorality.

SEX IS A GIFT FROM GOD

Daughter, I want to make it clear to you that sex is good. It is holy and righteous. God created sex. It is a gift from Him to us. God gave it to us for both pleasure and procreation. God made us not just spiritual, emotional, psychological, and physical beings, but He also made us sexual beings. The first commandment in the entire Bible, Genesis 1:28, tells a man and woman to have sex: "Be fruitful and multiply." Sex is holy when placed within the confines of marriage. But outside of marriage, it is sin. The Bible warns against fornication, adultery, and sexual immorality. Sex is a beautiful gift from God, but it can become ugly and hurtful when used outside of God's will. The issues concerning sex are not about its use, but its misuse—and even abuse.

So, Daughter, when you are married, you need to handle your business with your husband. Your husband's number-one need is sex, and you must minister to that need. Columbia

University Vice-Chair and Professor of Surgery Dr. Mehmet Oz says that if a man goes from having sex once a week to twice a week, he increases his life expectancy by three years. Some wives are cutting their husbands' lives short. Sex exercises the brain, the heart, and the pelvis. When a man has sex twice a week versus twice a month, he is less likely to have a heart attack. According to various sources, when a man has sex once a week versus once a month, he experiences the same emotion as if he has received an increase in his income by fifty thousand dollars.

Sadly, for years the church, in many instances, has sent the wrong message. The strongest message from the church has been, "Don't have sex. No sex. No sex. No sex." That message becomes so ingrained in a young woman's mind that when she marries, she may still have a feeling of reluctance when it comes to sex. Sex is wonderful, holy, and righteous within marriage. Daughter, when you marry, you can do whatever you and your husband agree to do. You can have a good time with sex because it is a gift from God.

If he doesn't already understand, I would encourage you to help your husband realize that while sex is important to you, it is not about the quantity, but the quality. Be open and clearly tell him that *for you* it's not how often that you do it, but it's how well you do it. Open your mouth and communicate with your husband that you want to be touched, to be held, to be caressed. Let him know that you want to be complimented and to be spoken to with love, respect, and appreciation. It will take a conscious effort for both you and your husband to achieve a mutually satisfying sexual relationship.

OUR BODIES BELONG TO GOD

Even subconsciously, we have all been influenced by our culture to the point that we need sexual healing. When is that going to happen? It's going to happen when we understand 1 Corinthians 6:13, which declares that our bodies were not made for sexual immorality. They were made for the Lord, and the Lord cares about our bodies. God is the one who created your body. Fearfully and wonderfully you are made. When God created your body, He had a purpose and intent for it. When God saved you, he didn't just save your soul, but your mind and body as well. We can't say, "I can do whatever I want with my body as long as my soul is saved." Paul says that God also cares about your body, and your body was created for a purpose. God's intent is not that you use your body to engage in sexual immorality. It's made to serve God. It's made to glorify God.

The problem for many of us is that we get caught up in instant gratification rather than delayed gratification. We think that we have to have everything right now. We try to grow up so fast by engaging in sexual activity earlier than God intended. That's an attempt to achieve instant gratification, rather than learning the value of delayed gratification. We want sex on our own timetable instead of waiting to experience it when God plans and in a way that will bring honor and glory to Him.

While speaking about operating outside of God's plan, Dr. A. Louis Patterson, pastor of Mount Corinth Missionary Baptist Church in Houston, says that whenever there is temporary pleasure, it always leads to perpetual ongoing pain. But whenever there is temporary pain, it always leads to perpetual ongoing pleasure. This means that if you withstand the temptation to have sex outside of God's guidelines, it may be painful in that moment to say no, but by doing so, you are aligning yourself with God's purpose for your life—a purpose that will lead to enduring pleasure.

Sexual temptation is real. The only ones who don't understand that are those who have never been close enough in a relationship for those feelings to be aroused. In their January 2011 "Facts on American Teens' Sexual and Reproductive Health," the Guttmacher Institute reports that by age fifteen, 13 percent have had sexual intercourse; by age nineteen, that figure rises to 70 percent. Not surprisingly, nearly 750,000 fifteen- to nineteen-year-olds become pregnant each year. In fact, in the United States, young women nineteen and under are responsible for 10 percent of all births.

The reason for these statistics is that temptation is present. You want to do it. You want to please your boyfriend. It is painful to say no because it brings tension and denies your body what it wants most in that moment. It hurts! But that pain is only temporary. It isn't going to last forever, and if you endure the temporary pain, it leads to perpetual ongoing pleasure. On the other hand, if you ignore God speaking through your conscience and allow yourself to engage in sex, you will find that the pleasure is only temporary. My grandmother says, "Two minutes of pleasure can lead to eighteen years of pain."

But even if you avoid pregnancy, sexual immorality sets you at odds against God's plan for your life. Your body was created to serve God, but instead you have served yourself. Your body was intended to please God, but instead you pleased yourself. As a child of God, knowing that you have disappointed Him will lead to feelings of guilt, the lowering of your self-esteem, and the realization you have lost something of yourself that you can never regain.

WHOM WILL YOU PLEASE?

One thing I want to stress to you again is that even men who profess to love you may only want access to your body. Such a man will try to dehumanize you by treating you like a sex object. You will no longer be a subject, but an object. You will find yourself wondering, after he takes what he wants and leaves, how he can go home and sleep without any guilt. If he saw you holistically, as a human being—with heart, soul, and mind, it would trouble him to treat you badly. But when you become an object in his eyes, he isn't bothered about how he treats an object. Once he dehumanizes you, he can do anything to you and it won't get to him.

I went to the Super Bowl in Arlington, Texas, in February 2011. During that time, there was a crazy winter storm. It was the worst snowstorm in the DFW Metroplex in thirty years. Nine inches of snow fell in a very short period of time. The Dallas area couldn't handle that because it doesn't have the salt for dealing with ice or the trucks necessary for snow removal. When I went to school in Dallas years ago, even two inches of snow would shut down the whole city. This year's snowstorm prompted shutting down everything except the Super Bowl game itself.

Because they didn't have salt to put down on the streets to deal with the ice, the city used sand. City employees didn't have the proper equipment to handle the ice on sidewalks, so they used rakes to try to break up the ice. In place of snow shovels, they used garden shovels. I even saw them trying to use a leaf blower in place of a snow blower! They were unsuccessful in their efforts to handle the ice and snow because they didn't have the equipment that was intended for that purpose. In spite of all their efforts, the sidewalks were still slippery and people kept falling. Have you ever wondered why some people's lives are slippery and they keep falling? It's because their bodies were never intended for sexual immorality.

Not only were you created to walk in God's ways, but you also made a personal commitment to Christ. You believe that Jesus died on the cross. You believe that God raised Him from the dead. You have received Him into your life. You are a Christian. There is no other commitment that is going to be more important to you than your commitment to Christ Jesus. Don't you let a commitment to a boy, or to a man, become more important to you than your commitment to God. There are times when you please God that you will not please a man. And, there are times that when you please a man, you will not please God. I'm trying to get you to grow to the point that there is nobody more important to you than Jesus, and no relationship more important to you than your relationship with God through His Son. If that relationship is intact, when some young man says to you, "If you love me, you will do it," you will respond, "If you love me, you wouldn't *ask* me to do it. You wouldn't ask me to betray the commitment that I made to Christ."

BOUNDARIES DEFINE AND PROTECT YOU

Our commitment to Christ comes with boundaries. We must have boundaries in our lives. In their book *Boundaries*, psychologists Henry Cloud and John Townsend point out that boundaries define us. Let me illustrate. When you and a girlfriend are talking about boys, you refer to some boys as "brothers" and "friends," but you identify other boys as "thugs" or "dogs." You have placed them at two ends of a continuum because of their boundaries, or lack thereof. The things they do and don't do determine how you see them. Their boundaries define them. They are either friends or dogs—or somewhere in the middle.

Don't you think the boys are doing the same thing with the girls they date? A boy is defining you by your boundaries. How far you will go with him defines you. He will test those boundaries. If you keep your cookies in the cookie jar, you are defined in one way. If you are willing to be coaxed into sexual activity with him, you will be defined another way. So, when he and his buddies are talking, you are considered either a woman of virtue and purity, a slut and a whore, or something in between. How did he come to his conclusion? Your boundaries defined you. Your boundaries are established by what you allow: "You can do this, but you can't do that." "You can touch me here, but you can't touch me there." "You can hug me like this, but you can't hug me like that." "Kiss me here, but don't kiss me there!" Your boundaries should be based on your commitment to Christ and what will please and glorify Him.

Drs. Cloud and Townsend point out that boundaries not only define us, but they also protect us. When God tells you to keep your cookies in the cookie jar, it isn't because He doesn't want you to have a good time. It's because God doesn't want you to kill yourself while you are having a good time. Boundaries protect you.

Every sport has boundaries. You know, baby girl, that my favorite sport is basketball. In basketball, there is a penalty for the illegal use of hands. That's a boundary. One player can't touch another player in just any way or hold another player. Not only is there a penalty for illegal use of hands, but if a player gets too many of those, that player is automatically disqualified from the game. Here's what I'm trying to tell you: If there are boundaries to protect grown people playing basketball, how much more you need boundaries to protect yourself as you go through life. Don't allow an illegal use of hands. If someone commits too many fouls, that person disqualifies himself from having a relationship with you. If a man doesn't respect your boundaries, he isn't worthy of you.

In the Old Testament, a seventeen-year-old young man by the name of Joseph had big dreams. He was confident that he was going to be a successful man of authority and prestige. He believed that God had plans and purpose for his life. After Joseph experienced a challenging beginning, God began to take him up the ladder of success. Eventually Joseph found himself working for a leader in Egypt named Potiphar. Joseph was suddenly a man of power and influence since he ran Potiphar's household and all of his business. But while Joseph was serving Potiphar faithfully, Mrs. Potiphar tried to seduce this handsome, well-built man. She tried to get him to sleep with her. Joseph couldn't believe what was happening. Without any enticement on his part, he found this woman blatantly throwing herself at him day after day. Nowhere in the Bible does it say that Joseph didn't want to sleep with his boss's wife. It doesn't say that he was not attracted to her. It does not say that he was not tempted. What it says is simply that Joseph basically told Mrs. Potiphar, "I can't sleep with you because my master has been too good to me."

Daughter, that's the level of commitment I'm trying to get you to have with Jesus. Even though you think a man is fine;

even though you want to be with him; and even though you have a desire for sex, you can resist him because of the level of commitment you have to Jesus. You can say, "I can't sleep with you because Jesus has been too good to me." It's about commitment. It's about accepting boundaries. It's about knowing that if you step outside the boundary, there is going to be a penalty.

The Race Isn't Always to the Swift

In the Beijing Olympics, Usain Bolt destroyed everybody in the field when he set a new world record in the men's 100m. Then he did the same in the 200m. In that same race, a runner representing the Netherlands came in second and a U.S. runner came in third. Both of these men were disqualified, however, because they both inadvertently stepped on their inside lanes. They crossed the boundaries, so they lost the race. They *appeared* to be coming out ahead, but they didn't place at all. They *thought* they were going to celebrate victories, but instead they had nothing to celebrate because they crossed the boundaries. Two other runners, both Americans, took the silver and bronze medals.

What I'm trying to tell you, baby girl, is that I know you have some friends who are trying to grow up too fast. They are doing things to please the boys; they are having one-night-stands. They are experiencing instant gratification and seem to be having a good time. Right now, they do look happy, and they are having a good time. But it isn't going to be as rewarding as they think because they are going to get disqualified. They think they are winning the race, but they aren't even going to place.

In the Beijing Olympics, the person who *thought* he came in fourth moved up to second when the second-place runner was disqualified. And the person who *thought* he came in fifth place was rewarded with third place. These two took rewards home with them, not because they were the fastest, but because they stayed in the boundaries while others crossed them. Among your peers, it may look right now like the fastest ones are winning. But when the race is over, you will find that they have been disqualified, and those who were faithful to stay within the boundaries are the real winners. Keep your cookies in the cookie jar until the appropriate time, Daughter, and you will know that you are a winner.

The connection you have with the Lord ensures that you are a winner. When you gave your life to Jesus Christ, 1 Corinthians 6:15 says that you became part of the body of Christ. You and Jesus have a special intimacy; you are one in the Spirit. Verse 19 points out that your body is a temple of God, and the Holy Spirit of God lives in you. You and Jesus have become one. You have such a connection to Jesus that Paul says you should *never* connect your body with someone with whom Jesus would not choose to be connected. Know, too, Daughter, whenever you sleep with someone, you are not just sleeping with that man, but with his history. You are sleeping with everybody with whom he has slept. Jesus doesn't want to have any part of that! Your connection with Him is a part of your wholeness. It's part of your deliverance and purpose.

DISTORTED VIEWS LEAD TO DISTORTED LIVES

It is so important that you have a healthy view of sex. But part of our problem is that as a society, we have an unhealthy view of sex. Our minds have been so distorted by this world, so messed up by TV shows, movies, videos, and music. You may say that you would never download any porn, but you may be faced with it without making any effort. So much that is in movies today *is* porn. Television shows include porn, and so many music videos are pornographic. If we don't immediately "run from sexual sin" that we see or hear, as verse 18 admonishes, it gets into our minds and colors our thinking. Before we know it, our view of sex becomes distorted. That's why a 2003 Gallup poll shows that 70 percent of teens believe it is okay for unmarried couples to live together. When they get their values from radio, television, entertainers, athletes, and singers rather than from God, their views are bound to be distorted.

Our society's argument for supporting cohabitation is usually that it gives the couple a chance to see if they are compatible—if they are going to be able to make it as husband and wife. That argument, however, is flawed. Cohabitation cannot be compared with marriage. Marriage requires the total commitment of two people to each other. Cohabitation needs a commitment only for the moment. There is a sacredness about the marriage vows that is not a part of a relationship between two people simply living together. For two Christians to believe that it is beneficial for them to live together before marriage is ludicrous. You cannot understand the will of God while deliberately living outside the will of God. Why should God give us guidance for the future if we are defiantly disobeying Him in the present?

ALL MARRIAGES ARE NOT EQUAL

It is sad, too, that some young people don't want to get married because of all of the bad marriages they've seen. They may look at grandparents, parents, friends, and coworkers, as well as celebrities in the news daily, and say, "I don't want to get married because marriage is messed up. Most marriages don't make it, and relationships just get ugly. I don't want any part of it!"

It isn't marriage that is the problem; it's the people *in* the marriage. When two immature, self-centered people get married for all the wrong reasons, how can the marriage possibly succeed? Those rejecting marriage need to find a new model to observe. They need to find a husband and wife who love God, are filled with the Holy Spirit, and are living according to the biblical directives for marriage partners. They need to see what marriage looks like when the husband loves his wife the way Christ loves the church and the wife respects her husband and submits herself to him as she does to Christ.

A couple weeks ago, I went to watch five- and six-year-olds play basketball in a children's league. It was the worst game I have ever seen in my life. The players would just pick up the ball and run with it. They would dribble, stop, walk, dribble, and stop. They would fall on the ball and just stay there, shoot air balls, throw in-air passes, and because they didn't know the boundaries, continually run out of bounds. At the end of the first quarter, the score was 2 to 0. Now, if I didn't know better, I could look at that game and say, "Basketball isn't worth anything. It takes no skill. The players just do whatever they want, and there is no teamwork at all. The whole thing is just crazy." But when I watch the Boston Celtics play the Los Angeles Lakers, I see how the game is *supposed* to be played. There is no comparison. *That* is basketball.

One of the things that helps ensure good playing at the pro level is the NBA's developmental league. When someone tries to go straight from high school or after one year of college into the pros, if that person isn't ready, he doesn't play. He goes down to the D league, where he can get more coaching, instruction, and opportunity to work on the required skills. He can also learn the boundaries. Then, when he is ready, he can move up to another level. Regarding marriage, we have too many people going from high school directly into marriage—with no coaches, no instruction, no discipline, no boundaries, no God, and no church. Then, when they fail, the blame is placed on the institution of marriage rather than on the immature and unprepared couple.

BE SURE THE SIGN IS STRAIGHT

Once when I had gone to Dallas to preach, I went running one morning and came across a sign by the Grapevine Mills Mall. It was supposed to be held by two screws—one at the top and one at the bottom. The top one, however, had come loose, causing the top of the sign to fall so that it was now upside down. An arrow directing travelers to Grapevine was pointing east, but I knew for a fact that it was actually west of that location. Another arrow indicated that to get to Dallas, travelers should go north, but I knew Dallas was actually south from there. The arrow marked "Exit" was pointing to the entrance of the mall. All of the directions were wrong because the sign was upside down. If I hadn't known my way around that area, I could easily have ended up lost. I would have mistakenly thought that I was going in the right direction, but I would have been wrong because the sign I was following was upside down.

In life many people think they are headed in the right direction, but they don't realize that there is something wrong with the sign they are following. Their guide is totally upside down, but they don't know that, so they keep following. They think they are going to reach their desired destination, but that is impossible because their instructions are upside down. It's an upside-down sign that says it's okay to have children before marriage. It's an upside-down sign that says cohabitation is equal to marriage. When we start accepting these distorted perspectives, we know we have watched too many television episodes of *Desperate Housewives, Sex in the City, The Bachelor* and *The Bachelorette, Who Wants to Marry a Millionaire*, and *Atlanta Housewives*, (who aren't even married to anybody in Atlanta!). We need to get back to listening to God, reading His Word, and looking to Him for our direction in life.

Daughter, keep your cookies in the cookie jar. If you don't, there is a huge cost. Not only would *you* pay the price in shame, guilt, and whatever other consequences might come from your behavior, but Christ paid an even greater price to give you the power to keep your cookies where they belong. First Corinthians 6:19-20 reminds you that you don't belong to yourself. You have been bought with a price. Jesus shed His blood on the cross to purchase you. He bought *all* of you: your body and mind as well as your soul. He paid dearly for you, child. Do what honors Him. You are His.

If We Fail, God Doesn't

There is one more thing that I want you to know about all of this, baby girl. If I haven't reached you soon enough with this talk; if you have *already* shared your body with someone; if you are even now weighed down by a guilty conscience, I want you to know without any doubt that I love you and God loves you. The same God who set the boundaries for our good is the One who offers us forgiveness when we cross those boundaries.

Acts 13:22 says that God identified David as "a man after my own heart." But David sinned sexually when he committed adultery with Bathsheba. After his sin came to light, David repented and prayed:

> Have mercy on me, O God, according to your unfailing
> love; according to your great compassion blot out my
> transgressions. Wash away all my iniquity and cleanse
> me from my sin. For I know my transgressions, and
> my sin is always before me. Against you, you only,
> have I sinned and done what is evil in your sight.…
> Create in me a pure heart, O God, and renew a steadfast
> spirit within me. Do not cast me from your presence
> or take your Holy Spirit from me. Restore to me the
> joy of your salvation and grant me a willing spirit, to sustain
> me. Then I will teach transgressors your ways, and sinners will
> turn back to you. Save me from bloodguilt, O God, the God
> who saves me, and my tongue will sing of your righteousness.
> O Lord, open my lips, and my mouth will declare your praise.
> You do not delight in sacrifice, or I would bring it; you do not
> take pleasure in burnt offerings. The sacrifices of God are a
> broken spirit; a broken and contrite heart, O God, you will
> not despise.
>
> PSALM 51:1-4, 10-17

My daughter, if you confess your sins even as David did,
you will find God just as faithful as David did. A broken spirit,
and a broken and contrite heart, God will not despise. His arms
are already outstretched, waiting to enfold you, waiting to forgive
you, waiting to comfort you. Walk in His forgiveness and let
Him restore to you the joy of your salvation. Trust Him, baby
girl. He will never fail to keep His promises.

CHAPTER 3

Handle Your Brain

Free Your Mind
and the Rest Will Follow

Do not conform to the pattern of this world, but be transformed by the renewing of your mind. Then you will be able to test and approve what God's will is—his good, pleasing and perfect will.

ROMANS 12:2

"MALE AND FEMALE HE CREATED THEM"

En Vogue was right: "Free your mind and the rest will follow." In Dr. James Dobson's book, *Bringing Up Daughters,* he talks about the uniqueness of a woman's brain. He notes that God has made your brain so very special. Your very DNA is different from a man's. Your chromosome pattern, as well as every cell of your body, are different. Unisex is a fallacy. There is no such thing as sexual universality; one MRI, CAT scan, or PET scan can prove that.

After eight weeks in the womb, the male brain is transformed by testosterone. The color of the brain changes, some of the communication cells are destroyed, and the emotional structure is changed. The transformations in the male brain are responsible for male aggressiveness. That's why boys run, jump, scream, rough house, and holler at the top of their voices.

The female brain, as Dr. Dobson points out, is not affected by testosterone in that way. The centers of communication and emotion become stronger, so girls are better able to express themselves verbally and emotionally. Baby girls are affected by the production of estrogen that enables them to enter into relationships with a greater sense of intimacy. Because of the way God made you and your female friends, you bond together as you talk about your feelings and the personal details of your lives. Men instead typically relate to one another on a much different level as they discuss sports, cars, politics, or some topic that does not involve their feelings.

The uniqueness with which God created women's minds explains why when Satan attacked the first woman, Eve, he attacked her in her mind, her thought process, the way she saw life. Genesis 3:1-6 records that incident:

> Now the serpent was more crafty than any of the wild animals the LORD God had made. He said to the woman, "Did God really say, 'You must not eat from any tree in the garden'?" The woman said to the serpent, "We may eat fruit from the trees in the garden, but God did say, 'You must not eat fruit from the tree that is in the middle of the garden, and you must not touch it, or you will die.'" "You will not certainly die," the serpent said to the woman. "For God knows that when you eat from it your eyes will be opened, and you will be like God, knowing good and evil." When the woman saw that the fruit of the tree was good for food and pleasing to the eye, and also desirable for gaining wisdom, she took some and ate it. She also gave some to her husband, who was with her, and he ate it.

The Bible says that Adam sinned deliberately. Even though he knew right from wrong, he was tempted by his wife's words and chose to eat of the forbidden fruit. But even Eve herself confessed that she was deceived: "The serpent deceived me, and I ate" (v. 13). She knew that God had said she and Adam were not to eat of the fruit from a particular tree, but the enemy manipulated her thinking and confused her. He caused her to question what God had said, and then assured her that her perception about the consequence for her disobedience was wrong. The enemy knew that if he could get her mind, everything else would follow. And it did. Her mind was deceived, so with her body she disobeyed God.

HEART FOLLOWS HEAD

It's really important, too, to see what happened when Eve's mind got messed up. It immediately showed up in her relationships. She first hurt her relationship with God. Instead of running to God, as she used to, she began running *from* God. She used to walk with Him and Adam in the garden, but now she feared God and hid from Him. Her relationship with her man wasn't the same. She used to be someone he trusted, but now he blamed her for their predicament (v. 12). She used to be totally open, vulnerable, and accessible to her husband, even as he was to her. Now they began covering themselves, concealing themselves from each other (v. 7). Eve's marriage changed. Her husband used to refer to her as "bone of my bone, and flesh of my flesh" (2:23). Now, when talking to God, Adam refers to her in an accusatory way: "the woman you put here with me" (3:12). As a result of Eve believing a lie, she lost her home and childbirth became a painful experience.

Daughter, Romans 12:2 tells us that God's will is good; it is even perfect. If Eve had just accepted the good and perfect will of God, things would have been so very different in her life. If she had just wanted for herself the same things that God wanted for her, things would have gone another direction. However, her mentality got messed up. She listened to the wrong voice and her perception changed. She began to think differently. Then, because her mindset had changed, she behaved differently.

Loving to Please Him

I was at the mall one day and saw a little girl who appeared to be about four years old. She and her father were having a wonderful interaction, and the connection between them was so amazing to watch. When they came across a rack of sunglasses, the father asked his little daughter, "Do you want a pair of sunglasses?"

"Yeah Daddy, I want some sunglasses."

"Which ones do you like?"

"Which ones do you like, Daddy?"

"Well, I like these right here. Try 'em on. How do they look to you?"

"How do they look to you, Daddy?"

"They look good on you. I like those. How do they feel to you?"

"Daddy, how do they feel to you?"

This little girl loved her father so much that she genuinely desired to please him. It wasn't a child who was *afraid* of displeasing her father or felt she *had* to please him if she wanted him to love her. Her desire to please him was simply her way of expressing her love to him. If he wanted something for her, then she wanted it too. If he thought something would be good for her, she trusted him so much that she believed it would be good for her, too.

That's what I desire for you, Daughter, in your walk with your heavenly Father. I want you to love your heavenly Father so much that whatever God wants for you, you want it for yourself. If God believes it is good for you, you also believe it is good for you. But remember that the enemy attacks your mind. He wants you to think differently from the way that God thinks, and to choose the opposite of what God would choose for you.

That's why the apostle Paul, in Romans 12:2, says, "Do not conform to the pattern of this world, but be transformed by the renewing of your mind." In other words, do not copy this world. Don't let this world shape you into its mold. Don't let this world squeeze you into its system. When the Bible talks about the world in this verse, it isn't talking about people as it is in John 3:16, which says, "For God so loved the world . . . ." Rather, it is talking about a system, or a culture. First John 2:16 says, "For everything in the world—the lust of the flesh, the lust of the eyes, and the pride of life—comes not from the Father but from the world." The lust of the flesh is craving that which will please the body, not that which pleases God. The lust of the eyes and the pride of life seek those things that are pleasing to self and that make one proud, not those things that please God.

THE PRESSURE MOUNTS

The world's system is at odds with the things of God. You must be careful not to let this system press you into a mold that will cause you to oppose God. The pressure that you so often feel is the world trying to force you to be like those whose allegiance is to this world—to dress like them, talk like them, act like them, and think like them. You are feeling the pressure of going against the crowd.

In the National Football League, all the teams have quarterbacks. Some say that Peyton Manning of the Indianapolis Colts is the best quarterback who's ever played the game. The opposing teams believe that if they can just put pressure on Peyton Manning, they can keep the Colts from getting to their goal. They know that Peyton Manning is too good for them to afford to let him sit back there in the pocket, pick the defense apart, and drive to the goal. They put pressure on him because they know if they leave him alone, he will beat them every time.

So how did they try to defeat Peyton Manning? They put pressure on him. There's a defensive end on the right side to bring pressure, and a defensive end on the left. There are line backers in the middle, and defensive backs to bring the blitz to pressure him right down the middle. What are they trying to do with all of that pressure? They're trying to force Peyton to do something he doesn't want to do. Or they hope to rush him into doing something he may want to, but not in that second. They are also trying to get Peyton to go out of bounds because if he operates out of bounds, whatever he does won't count. Why all this pressure? They are trying to keep Peyton from his goal.

Why has the enemy put *you* under so much pressure? Peer pressure is coming at you from the left; pressure from your friends on the right. Pressure to be accepted is coming up the middle. From all directions, there is pressure. Do you understand what it's about? This pressure is either trying to force you to do something you really don't want to do or rush you into something. There is something that you may want to do, but not now. You are waiting for the appropriate time, and this isn't it, but there is pressure on you to do it now. And then there is that pressure trying to force you out of bounds because if you act outside the boundaries of the will of God, whatever you do won't count. What's all this pressure about? It is a strategy of the enemy for trying to keep you from getting to the goal that God has for you.

With Peyton Manning, the opposition would like nothing more than to sack him—to tackle him before he has time to do anything significant with the ball. With you, Daughter, the opposition would like nothing more than to get you *in* the sack—to bring you down before you have a chance to accomplish significant goals with your life.

In order to protect Peyton Manning, the coach has provided for his protection. He's got an offensive line, including a center, guards, tackles, tight ends, and running backs—all to guard him so that he can get to the goal. God does the same thing for you. He has provided for your protection. You have parents who love you, a church that nurtures you, teachers with high expectations of you, and friends who hold you accountable—all to guard you so that you can reach the goals God has for you.

But you know that the opposition doesn't just see your protection and walk away in defeat. No, your opposition tries to get around your protection to put pressure on you. My wife Sharon made an important observation one day while watching football with me. We were watching highlights of Peyton Manning, and he was just eating up the opposition. He was slaughtering them—getting to the goal, making touchdowns, and taking his team to victory. But Sharon reflected as he let the ball go, "You know, the opposition isn't even thinking about him when he doesn't have the ball."

Daughter, have you ever wondered why you are under so much pressure? It's because you're seeking higher goals. You may see others around you who experience no pressure at all. They seem to have life so easy. The reason is that they aren't a threat to anyone. They aren't trying to do anything with their lives. They aren't striving for any goals that bring glory to God. The enemy isn't fighting them because he's already got them.

IN THE WORLD AND OF THE WORLD

There are characteristics that may be indicative of those who are part of the enemy's team. They may dress according to the dictates of the world, ignoring any thoughts about modesty or even appropriate dress. They may sleep with one person after another, not realizing that "just because they can" is not a good reason. They may be out of shape and think nothing of overindulging meal after meal, snack after snack. They may get drunk, dabble in pornography, or be totally self-absorbed.

Why all this negative behavior? Because they have been pressed into a mold. But they have no idea that this has happened. If you were to ask one of them, she would say, "I am my own woman." She doesn't realize that she makes decisions because of what she has seen on TV, or that she engages in certain behavior because of peer pressure. She doesn't realize that while she *thinks* she has her life together, her life is actually out of her control and she is being manipulated like a puppet by the influences in this world. She has been pressed into the world's mold and doesn't even know it.

Daughter, I want you to stop and ask yourself how strongly you are influenced by this world system. We all need to examine ourselves periodically. The influences of this world are insidious. They don't always confront us head on so that we recognize their strategies. Often we are exposed to *just a little* off-color humor, *just a little* porn, or *just a little* change in fashion. We don't have to be seeking these things; they seek us. One click on a website, and we find something that is totally unrelated to the search we were conducting. We immediately click it off, but what we have seen stays in our minds. We sit down to watch a new music video by some artist we have grown to appreciate, and suddenly there are words or images that we have never seen from that person before. You may pick up a women's magazine and see a cute little outfit that you know would look good on you, but you also know it reveals more than you believe is appropriate. Yet the temptation is there.

Most people who are under the spell of this world's system did not get there overnight. They were exposed to these things over time. If a girl eats one cheeseburger, it probably isn't going to affect her too adversely. But if she eats enough cheeseburgers over a period of time, she will find that it drastically changes both her physical shape and her life. She will find, too, that she can no longer eat just one cheeseburger. They have become part of her daily routine and she feels she has to have them.

That's what happens when people are exposed to pornography, godless philosophies, unhealthy relationships, etc. They don't see the changes in themselves as they are happening. But one day they wake up, look in the mirror, and ask, "How did I get in this shape? When did my little tastes of a cheeseburger become a craving? What has happened to me?"

You may ask, "What if I want to change the shape that I'm in? How do I do that?" If you're talking about eating too many cheeseburgers, you can't eat just one carrot and expect that to make a difference. You have to eat healthy foods over a period of time before you will see changes occur. You have to learn to choose what is healthy over what is unhealthy. It works the same way in changing the shape of your mind, changing your mentality. Instead of feasting on things that are not healthy for your mind, you must choose to internalize the holy things of God.

THE WORLD DOESN'T FIT YOU

Daughter, God doesn't want you to conform to this world. The American Standard Version translates Romans 12:2: "And be not fashioned according to this world . . . ." Why shouldn't you *fashion* yourself after this world? Because the world's fashion doesn't fit you. The preceding verse, Romans 12:1, says, "I beseech you therefore, brethren, by the mercies of God, to present your bodies a living sacrifice, holy, acceptable to God, which is your spiritual service." You have already done that, baby girl. You are a daughter of God. You have given your life to Christ. You have presented your body to Him and you are His. The things of the world don't fit you anymore. If you try to put them on, you find that the person you are on the inside is not compatible with the fashion of this world on the outside.

We've all seen people trying to dress in clothing that doesn't fit them. No matter how hard they try to make it work, it just doesn't look right. And it certainly doesn't feel right. The fashion they are trying to fit into was made for someone else, not for them. In the same way, you cannot fashion yourself after this world because it wasn't made for you.

Pastor Joy Thornton, of Greater St. Mark Missionary Baptist Church in Indianapolis, tells about going shopping one day in Atlanta when he was a young man. He came across a pair of shoes that he thought looked awesome. He was determined to have those shoes. So he asked the salesperson if he had them in a size 10.

The salesperson replied, "No, but we've got them in a 9."

"I don't wear a 9; I wear a 10."

"But we don't have them in a 10, only in a 9."

"Okay, give me the 9. These look so good. I want these."

He knew the shoes would be a size too small, but he was thinking, "I know a man in Indianapolis who knows how to stretch shoes. I'll make them work." So he brought them home and asked the man to stretch them. The man did his best, and they did stretch a little bit, but not nearly an entire shoe size. But he loved those shoes, so he wore them anyway. So here it is, all these years later, and Pastor Thornton said his feet *still* hurt. God gave him size 10 feet, but he insisted on making them fit into size 9 shoes.

It works the same way in other areas of life. If God has made you a size 10, you can't fit into a size 9 relationship. No matter how good it looks, it isn't going to work for you and will only leave you in pain. If God has created you for a size 10 destiny, you can't be satisfied trying to make a size 9 life work for you. It won't. It will only leave you wishing you had waited for the life that you were destined to have.

VICTORY THROUGH TRANSFORMATION

But just as those shoes were so tempting to Pastor Thornton, you will constantly be tempted throughout life to settle for less than what God has for you. So how do you overcome that temptation? How do you avoid being conformed to this world? You do it by being transformed. What do we mean by "transformed"? The word "transform" comes from the Greek word "metamorphosis." A metamorphosis is a change, but not just a common change; it's a drastic change—a radical change. If anyone be in Christ, he or she is a new creature. We cannot enter into Christ and have Christ enter into us and remain the same. Old things pass away and everything becomes new. God isn't looking for us to turn over a new leaf, but to become a whole new tree.

A good way of visualizing a metamorphosis is by looking at the transformation of a caterpillar into a butterfly. One day we see a wormlike little creature slithering in the dirt. But, impossible as it seems, the next time we see it, it's a beautiful butterfly soaring in the sky. That's the kind of metamorphosis God wants to make in our lives, baby girl. To stay in the world is to remain a caterpillar. To be a new creature in Christ is to spread our beautiful new wings and soar to new heights.

The verse we are looking at makes it clear that this metamorphosis comes about by the renewing of our minds. You may wonder what's wrong with the mind you've got now. The problem is that throughout our lifetime, we have been pressed into the mold of the world. Our minds have learned to think as the world thinks. That means our minds are full of preconceived thoughts—others' thoughts that we have subconsciously adopted without ever thinking for ourselves.

WHO DOES YOUR THINKING?

Some people think they know everything because they believe whatever the world has told them, just as Eve believed what the serpent told her. Instead of believing God, who told her not to eat a certain fruit or she would die, she believed a snake. The snake told her, "No, you're not going to die. You are going to become like God, knowing good and evil." From that day forward, instead of accepting God's view about what is good and what is evil, people have been deciding for themselves what is good and what is evil, what is right and what is wrong—regardless of what God says. That's an unsafe way to think and live one's life.

Those who leave God out of their thinking *believe* they are thinking for themselves, but in reality, they are merely accepting what the world says because the thoughts of the world are subconsciously embedded within us. With every TV show, every movie, every video, every commercial, every radio program, every magazine, we are filling our minds with what the world believes. We go around saying, "Well, *I* think . . . ," when all we actually know is what we heard some celebrity say on TV. Or, "*I* always buy X brand because . . . ," and we say what we heard on some commercial. Or even more frightening, "*I* know that . . .," because we have listened to some talk show personality pontificate on a topic and we have bought into the hype without ever listening to opposing views or researching the matter for ourselves. So many people *think* they are so knowledgeable when they really are full of ignorance.

But *thinking* they know everything makes them arrogant and hard to get along with. They can't have a genuine conversation with anyone because they won't listen to others. They spout their views and dismiss anyone who doesn't agree with them. First Corinthians 8:1-2 says, "But knowledge puffs up while love builds up. Those who think they know something do not yet know as they ought to know." Knowledge is a good thing, a positive thing, when it's based on God's Word, on the truth. When we seek truth and knowledge outside of God, we end up as "those who think they know something [but] do not yet know as they ought to know."

You cannot know everything, baby girl. You don't automatically know what it's like to be a Christian woman. You don't automatically know how to be a friend. You don't automatically know how to be in a relationship. You don't automatically know how to be a wife. You don't automatically know how to be a mother. You don't automatically know how to raise children. You don't automatically know about a career. You don't automatically know everything. But, if you *think* you know everything, you are not open to anything. It's especially important that you stay open to the Word of God, and allow God to speak to you, allow God to transform your mind.

DON'T LIVE DOWN IN THE DUMPS

Some women even let the world form their own self-image. The world has caused them to think a certain way about themselves. Models and stars are featured in women's magazines and are filmed walking down a red carpet, and they are each put on a pedestal as the "ideal woman." Many women who watch them then look at themselves in a mirror and feel bad about themselves. Then, they project onto others what they think about themselves. They think they are too tall, too big, or too flawed to be attractive, so they project those thoughts about themselves onto others. They think to themselves, "He thinks I'm too big" or "He thinks I'm stupid." They don't actually know what the other person thinks, yet they project their own negative perceptions onto that person. Whatever they believe about themselves, they think others believe it as well.

Daughter, don't let the pessimism that plagues this world become part of your mindset. Don't be like those who think everything is bad, and everybody is wrong. They don't like themselves and they don't like anybody else. They can't see anything positive. Wallowing in self-pity, they have no desire to get out of the mire. They dwell on the negative and turn everything into something bad. No one ever satisfies them. Nothing good ever happens to them. If anything positive appears in their lives, they quickly dismiss it by saying, "It won't last," "He won't stay with me," or "My employer has it in for me." The glass is always half-empty, never half-full. The world has pressed this person into its mold, and they are disregarding the principles of God.

PRINCIPLES THAT NEVER FAIL

The principles of God are like the laws of science and nature. The laws of science and nature do not take into consideration how much money you make, or your relationship situation. They work consistently. Gravity works all the time. It works for a single parent, and one in a two-parent household. Gravity works the same for those in poverty as for the wealthy. It works the same for women as for men. It works regardless of a person's state of mind or even what the person says he or she believes about gravity. It just works.

The principles of God are like that. They are consistent. They work for everybody. You need, therefore, to put those principles to work in your life. If you fail to do that—if you fail to believe God's principles, God's truths—you will develop a perverted mentality, a distorted way of thinking. Romans 1:28 says that there are those who "did not think it worthwhile to retain the knowledge of God, so God gave them over to a depraved mind." Why? Because when you suppress the truth of God, the only thing that remains is a lie. For instance, Deuteronomy 6:4 says, "Hear, O Israel: The LORD our God, the LORD is one." If you suppress the truth about God being only one God, you start believing there are many gods, or there is no God.

In John 14:6, "Jesus answered, 'I am the way and the truth and the life. No one comes to the Father except through me.'" If you suppress that truth, you start thinking that there are many paths to God and that you can get to God without Jesus. Hebrews

13:4 says, "Marriage should be honored by all, and the marriage bed kept pure, for God will judge the adulterer and all the sexually immoral." If you suppress the truth about marriage, you start believing that extramarital affairs can be okay and that sleeping together before marriage is just a natural part of dating. Why do people believe those lies? Because they have suppressed the truth. When we suppress the truth, the only thing that remains is a lie, and a perversion of our mindset. We start believing the truth is a lie, and a lie is the truth. We believe good is bad, and bad is good. We believe right is wrong, and wrong is right.

PITY THE PITY PARTIER

Another indication that we need a mindset change is when we start throwing pity parties for ourselves. What a pitiful mentality that is! We feel sorry for ourselves and we extend invitations to others to feel sorry for us. If they refuse to participate in our party, we get angry and pity ourselves all the more: "Nobody likes me. Nobody cares about me. Nobody wants to be with me." If we don't even want to be around ourselves, how could we expect others to want to be with us? Some people can't stand to be alone for five minutes. They feel that they have to *do* something or find somebody to be with, or they're going to go crazy. Some women are looking for a man to marry them because they don't want to be alone. But if they don't want to be alone with themselves, what makes them think some poor man is going to want to be with them? Why would anyone want to be around somebody who is constantly whining and complaining?

People who are constantly throwing pity parties don't care about anyone other than themselves. This is evident not only at a personal level, but even at an international level. There is a civil war going on in Libya right now. People are dying. Husbands, wives, sons, and daughters are being killed. But, as I heard NBC news anchor Brian Williams point out, the only concern being expressed by some U.S. citizens is how this war is affecting their gas prices.

Do you think, Daughter, that people who aren't even concerned about a civil war in which people are dying are going to be concerned about a civil war going on inside of you? They will only be concerned to the extent that your pity party is adversely affecting them. They won't come rushing to comfort you or help you. They will ostracize you and talk behind your back about how whiny you are and how you are no fun to be around. Pity parties never help their hosts to get what they want; they only alienate those whom they would like to have in their lives. If you have any tendencies toward self-pity, baby girl, get rid of those now. Change your mindset and how you operate in this world.

Love Sometimes Waits

Dr. Theron Williams once pointed something out to me from *Ray*, the movie about the life of Ray Charles. I had always thought Ray Charles was born blind, but he wasn't. Ray Charles became blind as a child when his eyesight gradually left him.

As this was happening, his mother told him,

"The doctor said you're going to go blind."

"I know, Mommy."

"You're not going to be able to see."

"I know."

Little Ray began crying and crying. His mother let him cry

because that's something to cry about. He was a little child, and he couldn't see. That's reason to cry. So he cried and cried. But then his mother said, "Okay, that's enough of that. You stop that crying, 'cause ain't nobody going to feel sorry for you 'cause you can't see. Ain't nobody going to feel sorry for you 'cause you're blind."

Then his mother led him over to the steps leading up to the porch. "Walk up these steps. How many steps was that from the ground to the porch?"

"Three, Momma."

"You better remember that, 'cause ain't nobody going to feel sorry for you 'cause you can't see. Now, how many steps from the porch to the house?"

"It's four, Momma."

"Don't you forget that, 'cause ain't nobody going to feel sorry for you 'cause you can't see. You better learn how to see with your hands and you better learn how to see with your ears 'cause ain't nobody going to feel sorry for you 'cause you can't see."

Ray's vision changes until one day he's completely blind. He's still just a little boy, but now he is blind. He's in the living room messing around. He trips and falls. "Momma, Momma," he cries. She's in the kitchen. She hears him calling for her. "Help me, Momma, help me! Momma, Momma!" His mother starts to rush to him, but she stops in the doorway leading from the kitchen into the living room. She just stands there. "Momma, why won't you help me? Pick me up, Momma!" She's crying now. Tears are falling down her face. She puts her hand over her mouth. She doesn't want her son to hear her crying. "Momma, Momma!" She doesn't move. She doesn't pick him up. She's got the strength, the capability, and the power, but she won't pick him up.

Then he stops crying. He hears a grasshopper under the chair.

He picks it up in the hollow of his hand. He listens to it. He hears a cow bell outside. He hears the crackling of the wood in the fireplace. He gets his hand close to it, and then he pulls back. He hears water boiling in the kitchen. He says, "Momma, I know you hear it, too. You're standing right there." And, while he's on his knees in front of his mother, she picks him up.

Why didn't she pick him up sooner? Why didn't she pick him up when he first fell? Why didn't she pick him up when he first started crying out? She was trying to stretch him in other dimensions so that he would learn how to see with his hands and see with his ears. She was trying to get him to experience things that he wouldn't have experienced if she had picked him up too soon. In order to empower him, she left him down there till he learned his lesson.

Why didn't God pick *us* up when we first fell? Why didn't God pick us up when we first messed up? Why has God left us in the mess we are in? It isn't because He doesn't love us. It isn't because He is too far away to hear our cries. It's because God knows we need to learn something. He's trying to stretch us, baby girl. But once we learn our lesson and we're on our knees before God, God will pick us up again.

THINKING AS CHRIST THINKS

"How do I do it?" you ask. "How do I transform my mind?" Philippians 2:5 (KJV) says, "Let this mind be in you, which was also in Christ Jesus." Our own minds have become too pitiful and too perverted with too much projection and preconceived foolishness. We need the mind of Christ. Romans 12:2, quoted at the beginning of this chapter, says, "Do not conform to the pattern of this world, but be transformed by the renewing of your mind. Then you will be able to test and approve what God's will is—His good, pleasing and perfect will." When our minds are renewed and we are transformed, then we can know God's will. We won't be using our own warped thinking to determine right from wrong, good from evil, or God's will from our own will. Our renewed minds will allow us to know God's will.

Verse 3 says, "For by the grace given me I say to every one of you: Do not think of yourself more highly than you ought, but rather think of yourself with sober judgment, in accordance with the faith God has distributed to each of you." The writer is telling us to have an honest assessment of ourselves. We shouldn't think too highly of ourselves, but neither should we have a negative self-image. This is so important, baby girl, because how we feel about ourselves determines our relationships. If we think too highly of ourselves, then we start thinking that we are better than others. We start looking down on those around us and develop a mentality of superiority. We would never say it, but if we think we are superior, then we relate to others as inferior.

If we think too lowly of ourselves, we'll become doormats and let others walk on us. Especially when women feel they are inferior, instead of waiting for the man of their dreams, some of them will let a thug or dog into their lives because they think that is all they can get—all they are worthy of having. Baby girl, make an honest assessment of who you are. How do you come to that honest assessment? Note in verse 3 that it says, "in accordance with the faith God has distributed to each of you," or the King James Version says simply, "by the measure of your faith."

You determine your value by the measure of your faith. It's your relationship with God, not your relationship with a boy or a man, that determines your value. You're not important because you hold the arm of an important boy, or significant because you hold the arm of a significant man. You are important and significant because of your relationship with God. You weren't born inferior, waiting for a man to come along and give you value. You were born as a child of God. Your value comes from your heavenly Father; you are a daughter of the King. Your worth is independent of any man. If you enter into a relationship with a man and that relationship doesn't work out, you are of no less value. He didn't bring your significance in this world and he can't take it away.

An honest evaluation of yourself has nothing to do with what you drive, how much money you make, what degree you earned, the size of your house, or the job you hold. It's the measure of your faith that counts. You can have a little car, but a big Christ. You can have little money, but a big Messiah. You can have a little house, but big hope. It's the faith that God has given you that allows you to honestly evaluate yourself.

Romans 12:10 says, "Be devoted to one another in love. Honor one another above yourselves." The world tells us to look out for Number 1, look out for ourselves. The world tells us to get all we can, can all we get, sit on the can, and poison the rest. The world assures us that it's all about us. But when we become Christians and take on the mind of Christ, our priorities and values change. Now, with the mind of Christ, we esteem others greater than ourselves. This isn't so difficult to do if we have made an honest evaluation of ourselves so that we know who we are and recognize our own worth. It isn't hard for us to celebrate someone else because that in no way diminishes us. For us to honor another person and put another above ourselves takes absolutely nothing away from who we are or our own significance or value.

HONORING OTHERS HONORS YOU

Be careful, Daughter, that you don't join in with a gossip group. Don't talk about your sisters behind their backs. Don't smile at their faces and then stab them in their backs with rumors or innuendos. Some people think that by putting others down, they are somehow lifting themselves up—that by degrading others, it will upgrade them. But that isn't how it works. When we put others down, it only makes *us* look more pitiful and less attractive ourselves. Baby girl, learn to honor others and prefer others above yourself. That is the mindset of Christ. It's a new way of thinking in this world, and if you haven't been practicing it, it may seem awkward at first. But let that become your lifestyle—not something you do one time, but something you do over and over again.

Most sisters have a problem with self-esteem, so let it be your goal to help build them up. Celebrate what you see in them and the good things you see them do. Dr. Frederick D. Haynes III, pastor of Friendship-West Baptist Church in Dallas, said, "If you don't hate, but you celebrate, God might let you participate." The late Dr. Caesar Clark said that "praising other people is kind of like perfume: you can't put some on them without getting a little on yourself."

By honoring others above yourself, you don't get caught up in jealousy and envy. Baby girl, that's ugly, and it doesn't fit you. If you become jealous or envious of another sister because of what she drives, what she wears, the man she's got, her house, her children, her career, and all of that, you really don't have an issue with her, but with God. What you're essentially saying is, "God, You don't have enough wisdom to know how to distribute Your blessings properly. Otherwise You wouldn't have given her a BMW and me a broken-down, beat-up hooptie."

Every good and perfect gift comes from above. So, whatever gift she has, she got it from God. Therefore, if you're jealous and envious of that, you're saying God doesn't know what He's doing. My daughter, God knows exactly what He's doing. You have no reason to be envious and jealous. When God gave her that house, that wasn't God's last house. When God gave her that BMW, that wasn't God's last BMW. When God gave her that job, that wasn't God's last job. When God gave her that man, that wasn't God's last man. Wait on the Lord, and esteem others above yourself. It's a different mindset. It's a different thought process. But if you keep doing it over and over, it begins to shape you into the person God wants you to be.

Do It Yourself

And then, what else do we need to do to renew our minds to be more like Christ? Romans 12:11 (KJV) says, "Not slothful in business; fervent in spirit; serving the Lord." That means no laziness—being willing to work hard, and keeping in mind that it is the Lord we are serving in our work. God worked six days and rested on the seventh. We have been created in the image of God. So, if God worked six days, we shouldn't be slackers. Some women sit back, thinking that some man is going to come along and provide for all of their needs. But God's instructions were not directed only to men. Women also need to work hard in school; work hard in their studies; work hard on their jobs; work hard on their career goals; work hard to achieve their dreams;

work hard on their friendships; work hard on their relationships; work hard in their marriage; work hard raising their children; work hard in their community; work hard at their church. Slothfulness, or laziness, is one of the seven deadly sins. God wants His daughters, as well as His sons, to work hard. He doesn't want His daughters lying around all their lives, waiting on a man to come and pay their bills.

I don't want my daughter to think that she has to wait on a man to get things to happen in her life. A woman waiting for a man to ride up on a white horse, enter into her predicament, and resolve all of her financial and other issues is like waiting for a fairy tale. Baby girl, men want the same thing women want. A woman wants a man who is doing something with his life and working hard to accomplish his goals. A man wants a woman who is doing the same thing. A man of purpose won't be attracted to a woman who has nothing to show for her life. A hardworking man won't be interested in connecting with a lazy woman. A man living his life to please God won't be drawn to a woman who is ignoring God's instructions and doing nothing to please Him.

Don't wait, Daughter, for a man to bring you what God will give you directly. You can get your own degree, your own job, your own business. You can make your own money, buy your own house, and purchase your own car.

Only Hard Workers Need Apply

One of our church members was giving back to the community by mentoring some young girls from broken homes. As she was talking with them one day, she asked the group of girls what they wanted to be when they grew up. One of them responded that she wants to be a doctor; another, a lawyer; another, a teacher; others wanted to be an athlete, a minister, and a principal. They all shared their dreams.

Then one of them said, "When I grow up I want to be the wife of an NBA player." That's her goal; that's her dream. Out of all the things in the world she could do, she wants to be the wife of an NBA player. Does she know there are only about four hundred and fifty NBA players in total, and a very long line of women ahead of her who also have that aspiration? And some of them actually *know* an NBA player. Has she ever asked herself what such a person would be looking for in a wife? These men who have reached the pinnacle of their profession understand discipline and hard work. Why would they want somebody who has done nothing with her life, who is totally lacking in self-discipline, and who avoids work as much as possible? Such a person would not add anything to their lives but would merely be a leech, draining them of their resources. I'm sure she must have gotten her idea from watching *Basketball Wives* on television. At first it was just a notion, but then it got her mind stirred up and she traded reality for a fantasy.

But let's give this young woman the benefit of the doubt. Let's say it isn't really a life of glamour and celebrity that she is seeking. Maybe her heart's desire is simply to be a full-time homemaker, so she is thinking that if she marries a man with money, it will allow her to fulfill her desire to stay at home and be the best wife and mother she can be. There is nothing wrong with that desire to devote herself to caring for her husband, children, and home without competing demands for her time and energy from a job outside the home.

But I wonder if this young woman has any idea how much it takes to truly be a homemaker. It doesn't mean sitting at home, watching *Desperate Housewives* while her husband is out working hard to support the family. Homemaking is hard work. A person can't be lazy and be a homemaker. A homemaker has to be a childcare provider, chief executive officer, strategic planner, teacher, psychiatrist, psychologist, housekeeper, nutritionist, chef, computer operator, laundry expert, nurse, law enforcement officer, counselor, financial analyst, interior decorator, pet caretaker, hair stylist, grocery shopper, facility manager, and a host of other things. No matter what field a person enters, it's going to take hard work.

Forgive, as Christ Forgave You

Another attribute of a renewed mind is harmony. Beginning with verse 14, the remainder of Romans 12 is about getting along with others. Romans 12:14-21 says:

Bless those who persecute you; bless and do not curse. Rejoice with those who rejoice; mourn with those who mourn. Live in harmony with one another. Do not be proud, but be willing to associate with people of low position. Do not be conceited. Do not repay anyone evil for evil. Be careful to do what is right in the eyes of everyone. If it is possible, as far as it depends on you, live at peace with everyone. Do not take revenge, my dear friends, but leave room for God's wrath, for it is written: "It is mine to avenge; I will repay," says the Lord. On the contrary: "If your enemy is hungry, feed him; if he is thirsty, give him something to drink. In doing this, you will heap burning coals on his head." Do not be overcome by evil, but overcome evil with good.

God wired our brains for harmony, for peace, for intimacy. He did not wire us for revenge. If we're going to let this mind be in us which is also in Christ Jesus, we have to learn how to forgive. That's what Jesus did. We cannot seek vengeance. We can't try to pay people back. We can't scheme and manipulate. No matter how much someone has hurt us, our only recourse is forgiveness. Some people think that by withholding their forgiveness, they are hurting their offender, but they are only hurting themselves. Someone has said that unforgiveness is like drinking poison and hoping your enemy will die. The world, with its bitterness and vindictiveness, is trying to squeeze us into its mold, but, as Christians, that mold doesn't fit.

One of the hardest offenses for a woman to forgive is one that was committed by the man she has loved. In a relationship, we become so vulnerable that our most sensitive areas are exposed. As we grow to trust the other person, we share more and more of ourselves. We allow ourselves to love that person with our inmost being. So, when *that* person hurts us, the wound is immediately deep and painful. Sometimes we think the pain will never stop. We think, therefore, that *this* type of wound, *this* type of offense, is an exception to God's rule about forgiving: "Surely, God wouldn't expect me to forgive *this*." But God does. We have to forgive. We have to let it go. We cannot tuck that offense inside of us and keep it as a grudge because it will only grow, fester, and poison our attitudes and our lives. We cannot repay pain for pain.

God says that we have to let it go and leave vengeance to Him. When we forgive, we are moving out of the way so that God can move into the situation and deal with it as only He knows how. He can bring to the light that which was done in the dark. He enforces His principle that we reap what we sow. He will take care of the matter if we leave it in His hands.

Do you think God is asking too much of us when He asks us to forgive? Think about Jesus, dying on the cross. He looked down upon the men who had lied against Him, beat Him, whipped Him, and hung Him on that cross. He looked down and saw His mother sobbing, and knew what this offense against Him was doing to her. He looked down and did not see most of His beloved disciples. Those with whom He had shared his most intimate thoughts and those to whom He had given so much had left Him when He needed them most. Jesus knew that from the moment He had come into this world, He had loved, healed, fed, and forgiven others. There had been no guile, no falsehood, and no sin in Him. He spent His entire life expressing love for our world, and our world crucified Him. With thorns in His head, nails in His hands, and spikes in His feet, Jesus responded to this hatred, pain, and betrayal by saying, "Father, forgive them."

His forgiveness did not end His torment. He still had pain. His forgiveness did not wait for His offenders to ask Him for that forgiveness. He offered it while His enemies were still jeering Him and waiting for Him to die, and while His "friends" were still in hiding, leaving Him to die alone. That's the mind of Christ, baby girl. Jesus didn't go to His Father with anger and bitterness in His heart. He let go of all that and committed Himself to His Father, trusting Him to make things right.

VICTIMS CAN'T FLY

Daughter, don't ever get caught up in living like a victim as some folks do. It will hold you back. It will make you unattractive. It will keep you from experiencing God's purposes for your life.

Guard against that, my child. People who choose to have a victim mentality have traded all that God had planned for their lives just for the right to have a continual pity party. They think others are looking positively on them and negatively on their offenders, but that is not true. They have become pitiful wretches who may get a moment of pity from others the first time they tell their story, but as their story is told over and over again, they are met only with disgust. Eventually they shrivel up and die alone because they have chosen to wallow in self-pity. Resist at all costs the temptation to embrace a victim mentality. Instead, rise up as the daughter of God that you are and declare your victory over your situation. Praise your God that He will see you through, and watch your life take on new meaning and purpose as you walk on in faith, believing that your Father has great things in store for you.

I was in Houston for a friend's funeral. As I made my way from the Galleria, where I was staying, toward the Fifth Ward I saw a woman's car on the side of the road in front of a gas station. The trunk lid of the car was up, and all of her stuff that apparently had been in her trunk was scattered all over the ground. I wondered why she was stranded there with the bunch of junk from her trunk lying all over the ground like that. But, as I turned the corner, I could see that she had a flat tire. Wherever she was going, the tire went flat on her, so she couldn't get to her destination. She was stranded. Then I realized that the reason her trunk was open and her things were lying out on the ground was because she had to get out her spare tire that had been lying under all those things in her trunk. In order to get what she needed so that she could make the change and be on her way again to her destination, she had to first get all of that junk out of her trunk.

Baby girl, the reason some women aren't going anywhere in life is because they refuse to get rid of all the junk they've accumulated. They were on their way, but something went flat, so now they're just sitting there, going nowhere, because they refuse to open up. They aren't willing to get rid of the junk: the unforgiveness, the grudges, resentment, and bitterness. Yet it all has to come out. Some women are living out of their trunk. They are living on all that junk.

It's time for these women to stop all their manipulation. They have to stop calling the man who left them. Stop writing him. Stop texting him. Let it go. Stop blogging about him. Stop trying to hit him up on Facebook. Let it go. Stop tweeting him. Stop showing up at his job. Stop following him around the city. Stop sitting in the parking lot at his apartment, trying to see who is coming and going. They need to let it go!

Baby girl, if you've got any junk you've been holding onto, please let it go. Open up to God and let it all out. If you need to, find a Christian counselor and open up to her or him. Don't let all that stuff keep you from moving on to God's destination for you, to God's purpose for your life. Be transformed by the renewing of your mind so that you can prove what is the good, the perfect, and the acceptable will of God. Free your mind of the junk and let the mind of Christ come in like a refreshing breeze. It's time to be transformed. It's time for a metamorphosis. It's time to stop slithering in the dirt. It's time to start soaring like the butterfly God created you to be. Baby, God made you to fly!

CHAPTER 4

Handle Your Business

Girl, Get Your Money Straight

Who can find a virtuous woman? for her price is far above
rubies.

The heart of her husband doth safely trust in her, so
that he shall have no need of spoil.

She will do him good and not evil all the days of her
life.

She seeketh wool, and flax, and worketh willingly with
her hands.

She is like the merchants' ships; she bringeth her food
from afar.

She riseth also while it is yet night, and giveth meat to
her household, and a portion to her maidens.

She considereth a field, and buyeth it: with the fruit of
her hands she planteth a vineyard.

She girdeth her loins with strength, and strengtheneth
her arms.

She perceiveth that her merchandise is good: her candle
goeth not out by night.

She layeth her hands to the spindle, and her hands
hold the distaff.

She stretcheth out her hand to the poor; yea, she
reacheth forth her hands to the needy.

She is not afraid of the snow for her household: for all
her household are clothed with scarlet.

She maketh herself coverings of tapestry; her clothing
is silk and purple.

Her husband is known in the gates, when he sitteth
among the elders of the land.

She maketh fine linen, and selleth it; and delivereth
girdles unto the merchant.

Strength and honour are her clothing; and she shall

rejoice in time to come.

She openeth her mouth with wisdom; and in her tongue
is the law of kindness.

She looketh well to the ways of her household, and
eateth not the bread of idleness.

Her children arise up, and call her blessed; her husband
also, and he praiseth her.

Many daughters have done virtuously, but thou
excellest them all.

Favour is deceitful, and beauty is vain: but a woman
that feareth the LORD, she shall be praised.

Give her of the fruit of her hands; and let her own
works praise her in the gates.

PROVERBS 31:10-31, KJV

THE FRUSTRATION OF NOT RECEIVING

Years ago I took my sons to a movie and we decided that, rather than getting a beverage from the cashier at the counter, we would get some juice from a vending machine in the lobby. The bottles of juice were visible in the vending machine, so while I was getting out the money, KJ, who was three years old at the time, was deciding just which kind of juice he wanted. I pulled some dollar bills out of my pocket, but they were wrinkled, so I was trying to flatten them and get the wrinkles out. In the meantime, KJ had made his decision, so he pushed the button to get his juice, but nothing came out. He pushed it a second time; nothing came out. He pushed it yet a third time; still nothing came out. He looked up at me and said, "Daddy, nothing's coming out." I replied, "Son, that's because you haven't put anything in."

Therein lie the frustrations in life. We see the advantages, opportunities, and possessions that exist, but we don't know how to acquire them. We see other people with them, but they have eluded us. We know what we want. We have pushed the right buttons—attending the right school, networking with the right people, choosing the right type of person to date, and going to a church where Jesus is exalted and the Word is explained. Yet, even with all of that, we still have not gotten out of life what we've been looking for. Baby girl, it is only when you put the right thing in that you can get the right thing out. And it is in the area of money, of personal finances, that most people fail to get it right; they don't have their money straight.

Some advantages, opportunities, options, and possessions will continue to elude you until you get your money straight. It doesn't matter who you know, what you know, where you go to church, or what has happened to you previously in life. Until you get your money straight, there are some things that simply won't happen in your life.

THE MIND-OVER-MATTER CONNECTION

Our previous discussion focused on getting your brain right, that is, becoming mentally in line with the Word of God. Even getting your money straight is dependent upon your mentality. Once your mind is liberated, your finances will follow. Let me explain.

Some people will always live in poverty and never have anything because they don't *think* they are worthy of having anything. They see others achieving goals and becoming prosperous, but they don't *think* they deserve to live like that. It's their mentality, their thinking, which is keeping them from living a fulfilled life. With that faulty mindset, even if they get something, they subconsciously spoil it for themselves. Rather than simply receiving good things with gratitude and praise to God, the inner thoughts of their minds tell them that they really aren't worthy of this, so their behavior follows that negative thinking. Without consciously realizing what they are doing, they sabotage themselves.

For instance, even a woman who loves God may continually find herself in relationships with men who are not seeking to please the Lord and do not even share her same values. Why? Because deep inside there is a voice telling her she doesn't deserve anyone better than this. Therefore, she doesn't even consider it possible that a good Christian man could be attracted to her; she fears being rejected by such a man.

Proverbs 31:10 asks: "Who can find a virtuous woman? for her price is far above rubies." Who can find a woman with strength and character? Who can find a woman whose value supersedes rubies and other expensive outward adornment? In fact, this Scripture is talking about a woman who is more valuable than anything she could put on—even the costliest gems. It doesn't say, "Who can find a woman whose price is as valuable as the jewels she is wearing?" No, her price is far more than any jewelry, clothing, or anything to do with her outward appearance. Her value rests in who she is, not in what she's wearing.

You've heard it said that "clothes make the man," but that isn't true for a man or a woman. Some women, however, are misled to believe that is true. They think their clothes make them who they are. Daughter, your clothes don't make you. Your jewelry doesn't make you. You are valuable, even invaluable, all by yourself. Jesus wore no kingly robes when He walked this earth, but He is the King above all kings. His value is in who

He is, not what He had on. That is true for you as well.

YOU ARE SOMEBODY

To recognize your value, however, you must know who you are. You are a daughter of God. You are a child of the King. You believe that Jesus died on the cross and that God raised Him from the dead. By your faith, He has already taken up residence within you. You are of great value because of who you are and your relationship with God. That is not dependent upon what you can or cannot afford to wear.

This woman of great value in Proverbs 31 has healthy relationships. Verse 11 says that her husband trusts her. He is enriched by her. His life is better because of her. He will never be poor because of her. She adds value to their relationship. Theirs is a healthy relationship. This man did not give her value to her. We see in verse 10 that she already had value before he is even mentioned in verse 11. What if he had not come into her life? She would not have lost any of her value. What if a man had shown up, but had abused her instead of appreciating her? His character and actions would not have diminished her value at all. She was somebody all by herself. The man did not make her who she was: God did!

Once you understand that, baby girl, that's when you open yourself up so that your relationships can begin to work out and your resources can begin to expand. You recognize that your dependency is upon God alone, and through Him you can live that abundant life Jesus said He came to provide for us. (See John 10:10.)

WAITING FOR A KING

Let me point something out to you, Daughter. Let me put Proverbs 31 in context. If you go back to verse 1, you will find that this chapter is a record of the words King Lemuel's mother taught him. Wanting her son to be a wise king, as well as one who would be at his best and prosper, she gave him her loving counsel. She was advising him not just as her son and not just as a man, but also as a king. In essence she was saying, "Son, you are a king. You can't live just any kind of life. You are not like everybody else. You have to be careful in all that you do and in all of the decisions that you make." Then she proceeded to tell him what sort of woman he should be looking for—as a king.

Daughter, some men want women with no virtue. They don't want women of value because then they would have to treat them differently. To their warped minds a woman without virtue can be used, abused, and tossed aside, but a woman of value would have to be respected and cared for in a special way. They aren't after a relationship because they don't want to take on that responsibility. They are living only for the moment, and when they are through with getting what they want, they will move on. They are not kings, my daughter, and if you connect with one of them, you will not be a queen.

Since you are a child of the King, you have queenly potential. You need to keep your virtue, keep your value, and wait for your king to come along. While you are waiting, keep in mind that you are waiting for someone worth waiting for—you are waiting for a king. If you wanted a court jester, you could be married anytime because they are plentiful. But kings are scarcer because they are of far greater value. Fools are everywhere because it costs nothing to be a fool. Anybody can be one. It doesn't require any time, wisdom, self-discipline, or thought. On the other hand, it takes time for a king to develop. Yet he will be worth the wait.

PRODUCTION VS. CONSUMPTION

While profiling the woman that her son needs, Lemuel's mother points out that she must be a productive woman. That is one of the traits of a woman who has great value. She isn't a woman who is just sitting around, waiting on some man to show up and do something for her. She isn't sitting in poverty, hoping that a man will come along and pull her out of her situation. No! Instead, she is a woman of action.

Look in Proverbs 31 at all the verbs connected to this woman. She: does good and not evil; seeks raw materials and works willingly; goes out and brings in food; gets up early and prepares meals for her family; considers business options and invests wisely; works outside in the fields; exercises physically to gain strength; is detail oriented in her work; willingly works late if she needs to get something done; sews and weaves; gives to the poor; provides clothing for herself and her family; looks for quality; runs her own business; speaks with wisdom and kindness; and refuses to be lazy. You can be sure this woman has her money straight. She has learned to be a producer. She knows how to make a profit. She works hard, but not just for herself; she works hard to make sure the needs of her husband, family, and others in the community are cared for.

Sadly, too many of us in America have become mere consumers, not producers. We run from store to store and mall to mall consuming what other people produce. We gauge our success by how much we consume. We think that because we have *things*, we are doing well. We don't realize that we are simply giving an appearance of something that is not true. We lease a car, rent an apartment, rent our furniture, and charge our clothes, and yet we like to think that we are successful.

According to the 15th annual "Buying Power of Black America," Target Market News reports that, in 2008, the earned income of Black consumers was $803 billion. But what we spent our money on is very telling about our priorities. Our expenditures included: $26.9 billion on apparel products and services; 31.5 billion on cars and trucks; 6.6 billion on personal care products and services; 8.3 billion on media; 3.1 billion on tobacco and smoking products; 2.8 billion on alcoholic beverages; 12.9 billion on household furnishings and equipment (not appliances); and 2.8 billion on entertainment and leisure, but only $289 million on books (http://www.targetmarketnews.com/storyid01201001.htm).

Unfortunately, there are women who will spend a hundred dollars every week to get their hair and nails done, but they say they can't afford to go to college. If they continue to spend that much over twenty years, they will have spent over a hundred thousand dollars to make themselves look good on the outside, but they will have neglected that which would have increased their value on the inside.

We must learn to be producers rather than mere consumers. By producing, I mean creating, manufacturing, building, generating, or styling something. When we produce, we are creating. It may be something we create using our hands; or, it could be something we create using only our brains; or it could be something we create using a special gift, such as music. Genesis 1 begins, "In the beginning, God created . . . ." We are made in the image of God, who is the Creator. When we are creating, we are portraying our likeness to the One who made us. Our spiritual enemy, on the other hand, is a consumer. John 10:10 points out, "The thief comes only to kill, steal, and destroy...," not to create. We are behaving more like him when we consume.

A MIXED-UP MENTALITY

What is ironic is that we want to get some sort of credit simply for our consumption of a product. Here's what I mean. A woman walks into a room wearing a new dress or suit designed by Donna Karan and expects to receive compliments. She isn't Donna Karan. She did not create that dress. She simply looks good because of someone else's creativity and productivity, and yet she will be hurt or offended if others don't acknowledge and praise her for what she is wearing. Why should she get the praise for simply spending money?

The same thing happens when someone buys an expensive new car. A man pulls into the parking lot in his new Lexus or BMW, proudly exits the car, and pauses momentarily to make sure he is seen. Sure, he has a great car, but why does he expect compliments or praise? He didn't make that car. He had nothing to do with its creation. All he did was spend his money to consume it. We need to learn how to be creative so that we will be a reflection of the God who made us.

Following a church service one Sunday, after I had used the car example in a sermon, a young woman came to me and verbally lashed out. "Pastor," she said, "I don't care what you say. I like my car. I just bought it. I worked hard to get this car. I sacrificed and saved until I could finally buy it. And I love my car." I responded to her, "I didn't tell you not to like your car. I didn't tell you not to save or not to appreciate the hard work you put into getting the car. I think that's wonderful. What I said was that you are riding around in somebody else's creativity." Then I told her, "Now, when you come back in a few years and tell me that you own the dealership, then we can hold another conversation." We have to move beyond being mere consumers.

Many people are living in virtual prosperity. They aren't prosperous; they don't even *own* anything. They have begun living in a fantasy world. It would be like someone who is playing tennis on a Wii with Serena Williams thinking that she is actually playing with Serena Williams. But it isn't true because it's just a game. It's *virtual* reality, not *actual* reality. Many people are renting their homes, and yet they live as though they own them. They reside there, decorate the space, and invite others over to visit them there, but the reality is that the place still isn't theirs. They only get to stay there because they give someone else money every month.

Someone can go to a game room, put on a special mask, and get the sensation of skiing down some snowy slopes in Aspen. But when she takes off the mask, she discovers she has gone nowhere. Her reality has only been virtual, not actual. Baby girl, I want more than that for you. I want you to actually go places and do special things during your lifetime. I want you to own more than you owe! But you can't do that until you learn how to produce rather than just consume.

LEARNING TO PRODUCE

The woman in Proverbs 31 has learned to produce. Just look at the following verses:

She selects wool and flax and works with eager hands.
She considers a field and buys it; out of her earnings,

she plants a vineyard. She sets about her work vigorously; her arms are strong for her tasks. She sees that her trading is profitable, and her lamp does not go out at night. In her hand she holds the distaff and grasps the spindle with her fingers. She makes linen garments and sells them and supplies the merchants with sashes.

(Proverbs 31:13, 16-19, 24)

She is a clothing designer. She works with wool and linen to make fine clothes for others to wear. She's creating, designing, producing, and selling her garments. She used her earnings to buy a field, but not so that she can just let it sit idle. No, she plants a vineyard in that field. She produces grapes that are used to make wine and grape juice. Clothing. Grape juice. Wine. This woman is producing what others consume.

If all we do is *need* what others produce, it costs us. But when we produce what other people need, it profits us. You might wonder how this woman knows how to do what she is doing. How did she become a clothing designer and seamstress? How did she know about operating a business? How did she ever figure out how to grow grapes? These are not things that she would have known from birth. No one innately knows how to weave cloth, design and sew clothes, operate a business, or grow grapes. She had to learn these things somewhere along the way. As a woman she probably didn't have any formal schooling due to the age in which she lived. But she didn't let that stop her from succeeding. Somewhere along the line, she was taught, trained, or mentored.

She may have been smart enough to pay attention as her mother taught her how to sew. She may have learned how to handle her finances from her parents and, undoubtedly, developed a positive work ethic by watching how they provided for their family. She may have learned about growing crops, even grapes, from her father, or by watching what some of her older brothers did as they each set out on their own. She didn't waste opportunities to learn. She didn't spend her time *fantasizing* about how she would someday like to own her own business or create her own clothing line or be a successful grape grower. Instead, she prepared herself in her present so that she could realize her dreams in her future.

She may have earned a pittance working as a child for a professional seamstress in the community. Other girls might have had that same opportunity, but they may have thought to themselves, "I'm not going to work for her for just pennies. She's not going to use me like that. I'm not her servant." But this girl's mindset would have been different. She would have thought, "Yes, I know I'm worth more than this, and I know she's taking advantage of me. But I'm the one who is gaining the most. I am using this as an opportunity to learn to do my very best at this job, even though it often seems dull and boring. Someday, maybe I'll be able to put what I'm learning to better use."

What happens to you someday, Daughter, when opportunities become open to you? Are you going to be prepared to take advantage of them? Are you going to be educated and trained to walk into them? What are you learning today that you will be able to apply tomorrow? What credentials can you present to a potential employer? What degrees have you earned? What natural talents have you developed? And, most importantly, when God calls you to serve Him in a specific way—as a teacher, a doctor, a preacher, a business woman, or whatever it might be—are you going to be able to respond immediately? Or will you have to say, "Sorry, God, I really didn't think I would need a college degree because I just wanted to get married and have kids. Wait for me to finish school, and then I'll do what You ask."

If you hesitate in getting an education, you will only find it more challenging to go back to school later on. A thirty-five year old woman who has a real talent for helping other women with their hair and nails may be working instead in a fast food restaurant because she is saying, "I really like doing hair and nails, but it's too late for me to go to school and get a license to be able work in a beauty salon." A woman in whom God has placed a teacher's heart may be thinking to herself, "I wish so much that I had graduated from high school and gone on to college. Now, I've got three children and my husband has walked out on us. I'll never be able to be a teacher. I know I could get my GED without too much time or effort, but what's the use? If I went on to college, I'd only be able to go part time. It would take me *ten* years to finish my degree. I'd be forty-nine years old!" Let me ask you something. If you don't go back to school and get a degree, how old will you be in ten years? Do you want to be forty-nine and still working for minimum wage in a job you hate, or do you want to invest your time and effort now so that when you are forty-nine, you will be realizing your lifelong dream?

DELAYED GRATIFICATION WINS

Let's look at the Proverbs 31 woman again to see how she reached such a high level of success. How was her virtue expressed in the area of finances? How did this woman get her money straight? She did it not only by working hard, but also by planning her purchases. In verse 16, we see that she "considered a field." She thought it over. She investigated the field, analyzed it, and checked it out. She took time to deliberate, to think it through, before she made the purchase. She wasn't an impulse shopper.

We know also from this verse that she used her own money to buy the field. She didn't just happen to see the field one day while she was out walking and say, "Oh, I have to own that field! Just look at it! I *need* this field!" She didn't indebt herself and her husband to something that she couldn't afford. She didn't let her children do without so that she could have something she wanted. No, she took time to plan how she would pay for the field, and then she decided whether or not she could afford that purchase.

Buying a field was no small purchase. She realized that if she bought the field, she would not be able to afford to buy other things. She would have to make her children's clothes rather than pay someone else to make them. Even though her husband was a respected man in the city, she would have to make her own bed linens. She would have to keep working hard if she were going to buy this field. But she was a woman with a plan. She knew that by sacrificing in the short term, she would be building wealth in the long term. Buying the field would allow her to start a second business. It would take time and considerable labor, but in the end it would pay off.

Some women are so different from her. They get a little money, and off to the mall they go. They don't come home until they have spent it all. They aren't thinking ahead or planning their purchases. They simply buy what they want. If they want a new dress, they get it. If they want new shoes, they get them. It doesn't matter that this will take them deeper into debt. It doesn't matter if they aren't saving for a rainy day. It doesn't matter if they aren't putting any money aside for their children's college education. It doesn't matter if the car needs some work or they haven't been to the dentist all year. All that matters is how they feel in that moment. And in that moment, they are thinking, "I deserve this new outfit. I work hard, and if I want something, I'm going to get it." Or if they have been impulse shopping so long, they don't even stop to think at all. Their brains are simply in a state of habitual numbness and they operate solely from base instinct.

BE A WISE CONSUMER

Daughter, there are at least three things I want you to think about before you make any purchase. First of all, consider the cost and value of the item. Is this item worth the cost? Is its value worth more than, or at least equal to, what you would be paying for it?

Then, also ask yourself, "Why am I buying this?" If you have ten suits but haven't worn five of them in the past two years, why do you want to buy an eleventh suit? If you have fifty pairs of shoes but keep wearing just your three favorites, why do you want one more pair? "Why am I buying it?" is even more important than "Can I afford it?" Are you buying it because you want other people to think that you're important and successful? If so, that's a self-esteem issue, not one that can be satisfied by having something new. Are you buying it because you think it will cause a man to be attracted to you? If so, that's a relationship issue, and only a superficial man would care more about what a woman is wearing than what is in her heart. Are you buying it because you feel empty inside? If so, that's a spiritual issue, and it can't be resolved by purchasing something material.

The third thing to think about is whether this purchase will satisfy an actual need or simply a desire, a want. A need is something essential. A desire is something you don't really have to have, but you want it anyway. For instance, you may need a car to provide transportation. The Hyundai Accent GL was one of the least expensive cars sold in the U.S. in 2011. It would satisfy the basic need for transportation. But someone who buys a Ferrari obviously desires something more than satisfaction of a basic need.

This doesn't mean that you always buy the least expensive item you can find. Determining quality, how long the item will last, and how much upkeep it will require are important considerations when determining the value of an item. But if you insist on buying things that you cannot afford, things that you *want* but you do not *need*, you will soon find yourself in financial collapse. We are talking here about financial planning. Your income must exceed your outgo. How much are you bringing in? What are your expenses now? What are your financial goals?

Notice, too, that the purchase made by our Proverbs 31 woman was for something that appreciated in value, something that would be worth more later on than when she bought it. She made her own clothes, made her own meals, and made items for her home. When it came to *buying*, she purchased land, real estate, something that would appreciate. As soon as we drive a car off the lot, it depreciates in value. No matter how much we pay for an outfit, if we try to resell it, we aren't going to get nearly what we paid for it. But land is something that is most likely to appreciate over time because it isn't being reproduced. No one is mass producing more land. God created what land there is on this earth and He isn't making any more.

THINK WEALTH, NOT MONEY

When we think about financial planning, we need to

understand the difference between money and wealth. Most of us are just after money. We want more and more of it. We get excited when we get more, but discouraged when we get less. What we don't understand is that money and wealth don't mean the same thing.

You need to learn how to make your money work for you to help you build wealth. You need to get professional help to learn about stocks and bonds. You need to know the value of putting money into an IRA or a 401K. You need to understand how owning a business and operating it wisely can increase your wealth. Remember, baby girl, money and wealth are not the same thing.

When Sharon and I first moved back to Indianapolis in 1988, we drove up in a Ford Mustang. It was already paid for. At that time we had only one son, so that Mustang met our needs. We didn't need a bigger car right then. But when I came to pastor Eastern Star Church, folks were telling me I needed to upgrade my car. They were saying, "You need a Cadillac," or "You need a Lincoln." Now, I couldn't afford a Cadillac or a Lincoln. But even if I could have afforded it, I wasn't going to get one. That was not my priority. I was a young man with a young wife and a young son. I wasn't focused on getting a better car every year. I was thinking about building wealth for my family, providing for their financial security. I knew that meant that I couldn't be a frivolous spender.

Sharon and I have only owned two houses. We lived in the first one we bought for eleven years. Friends, family members, and acquaintances were all upgrading their houses, and I understand the idea of selling a house for more than the purchase price and getting a nicer house. But our focus was on building wealth, not just getting a bigger and better house. We were trying to put enough money into our house to gain some equity in it. Then we eventually sold that house and had enough equity to buy a decent home, which we have lived in now for twelve years. Our next home is going to be a nursing home!

Why aren't we interested in working our way up to a mansion? Because we're building wealth instead. When we get money, we're investing it into something that will make more money. Let me explain it to you with the board game, Monopoly.

IMPORTANT LIFE LESSONS

Life, Scrabble, and Monopoly were some of the games I have played with my children over the years to help them think, learn, and grow wiser. Monopoly was one of my sons' favorites. When they were younger, they were always trying to beat me at it, but they couldn't. They woke me up one day, saying, "Daddy, come on. You want to play Monopoly?"

"Yeah, set it up. I'm coming."

"Daddy, we're going to beat you."

"You can't beat me. You don't even understand the concept of the game."

"Yes we do, Daddy. Monopoly is about mathematics."

"Monopoly isn't about mathematics. It's about economics. Until you know the difference between mathematics and economics, you will never be able to beat me."

As we started the game, everybody had the same amount of money, had the same opportunities, and had to play by the same rules. So we began going around the board. I began buying property and making investments. Why? Because I was building wealth.

What were they doing? They were just collecting cash. They couldn't wait to move around "GO" because they got two hundred more dollars. They were getting cash money, and they were excited! While my cash flow was dwindling because of my purchase of property, their cash was increasing. "Daddy, you haven't got much money," they observed.

They were right, but they didn't realize that I wasn't throwing my money away. I was increasing my wealth. I bought a piece of property; then I bought all of the property in that section. I had to be a little patient, but eventually, I could put a house on each of those properties, then another house, and another. Finally, I decided to take a chance and put a hotel on my properties because I was developing them. Then I got a monopoly on the utility companies because everybody had to go past the water and electric companies.

"Daddy, where's your money?"

"I don't have the money, son, but I'm building my wealth."

They didn't understand that. They wouldn't make investments. They wouldn't buy any property to develop it. Jordan, my second son, was trying to follow my example, but he didn't understand the pattern of economics. So rather than spend enough money to get good, sound property with some value, he was buying property in the ghetto. He bought Baltic Avenue, Mediterranean, Oriental, and that group. Now, even with property in the ghetto, you can make some money. But Jordan was just buying the property; he wasn't developing it. So I landed on his property and he proudly told me, "You owe me four dollars." But without developing his property, no matter how long we played, it never earned him more than four dollars when we landed on it.

With my understanding of economics, I bought Boardwalk,

Park Place, Marvin Gardens and that whole neighborhood, along with Illinois and that neighborhood. Next I used my money to put houses and then apartments on the property I owned. Eventually, because they wanted money and not wealth, I got all of J. Allen's property and money, all of Jordan's property and money, and all of Jalon's property and money.

You may be thinking, "That's really mean. You're an adult. You can't expect children to know as much as you do. Why didn't you let them win? Would it have hurt you to let them win?" No, it wouldn't have *hurt me* to let them win, but it wouldn't have *helped them*. If they didn't learn anything from playing the game, they wouldn't have any lessons to take with them into the real world. No one in the real world is going to *let them* win.

Jalon, the youngest in the game, became angry and began crying because he didn't win. I didn't apologize or feel sorry for him because no one in the real world is going to feel sorry for him or give in to him because he cries. My message to him, a lesson he needed to learn, was this: "Son, either learn how to play or stay out of the game." Daughter, that's my message to you now, too. Learn how to play this economic situation or stay out of the game, because no one is going to feel sorry for you if you lose.

THE ULTIMATE GOAL

Look at how the Proverbs 31 woman got her money straight. She planted because she understood the concept of sowing and reaping. After buying a vineyard, she developed it by planting and later reaping the harvest. But look beyond those first verses. When you go on down to verse 20, you see that she isn't just sowing in the soil, but she's also sowing into souls. She's helping the poor. She isn't gaining wealth just to buy things for herself. Her goal wasn't to become rich and selfish. Her goal was to give to the poor. She blessed those who were less fortunate. Look at what 2 Corinthians 9:7-9 says:

Each of you should give what you have decided in your heart to give, not reluctantly or under compulsion, for God loves a cheerful giver. And God is able to bless you abundantly, so that in all things at all times, having all that you need, you will abound in every good work. As it is written: "They have freely scattered their gifts to the poor; their righteousness endures forever."

The Bible is full of admonitions for us to give to the poor and to take care of "the least of these." This is one area in which secular financial counselors can lead folks astray. They are good at advising us about saving, investing, putting our money to work, preparing for retirement, and all that. But some of them don't understand God's principles. They don't know about reaping what we sow or about helping those less fortunate. They don't know that Jesus said, "Truly I tell you, whatever you did for one of the least of these brothers and sisters of mine, you did for me" (Matthew 25:40). Some will even advise you that you don't need to contribute anything unless it will be a tax break for you.

But you know God's principles, baby girl. Even when you are going through rough times, you will find others worse off than you are. If you really want to be blessed, go find somebody who is worse off than you and bless that person. In Deuteronomy 15:7-8 and 10-11, we see how God told the Israelites to behave when it came to caring for one another:

If anyone is poor among your fellow Israelites in any of the towns of the land the LORD your God is giving you, do not be hardhearted or tightfisted toward them. Rather, be openhanded and freely lend them whatever they need.… Give generously to them and do so without a grudging heart; then because of this the LORD your God will bless you in all your work and in everything you put your hand to. There will always be poor people in the land. Therefore I command you to be openhanded toward your fellow Israelites who are poor and needy in your land.

Proverbs 19:17 says, "Whoever is kind to the poor lends to the LORD, and he will reward them for what they have done." When we give to the poor, it is like lending money to God. Jesus tells us in Luke 6:34-35 that even if we are lending to our enemies, we shouldn't expect repayment: "And if you lend to those from whom you expect repayment, what credit is that to you? Even sinners lend to sinners, expecting to be repaid in full. But love your enemies, do good to them, and lend to them without expecting to get anything back." Yet the verse in Proverbs says that when we are kind to the poor, when we give to them, it is the same as *lending* to the Lord. When we give to the poor, the Lord obligates Himself to give back to us. *We* are not telling *Him* that He owes us something if we give to the poor. *He* is telling *us* that if we give to the poor out of kindness, He will consider that as a loan to Himself, and God will never be indebted to anyone. He will give graciously to those who have given compassionately to others.

Baby, don't ever say that you cannot afford to give. The fact is, you cannot afford *not* to give. When you bring your tithe to God, He opens the windows of heaven and pours out a blessing so abundant that you can't receive at all (Malachi 3:10). If you sow a little, you will reap a little. But if you sow a lot, you will reap a lot (2 Corinthians 9:6). Even if financial counselors don't talk about this when you hear them offering financial advice, you must remember that this principle holds true.

YOU CAN'T BEAT GOD GIVING

In 2006 Bill Gates expressed his frustration over being named the wealthiest man in the world, saying, "There's nothing good that comes out of that." But ever since he and his wife Melinda established the Bill & Melinda Gates Foundation in 2000, he has been learning that an incredible amount of good can come out of giving money away. Starting with a $28 billion endowment, they have given away billions of dollars to combat HIV/AIDS, fight diseases in third world countries, improve libraries and high schools in the U.S., provide funds for scholarships, feed the hungry, and help with many other causes.

In 2006 Warren Buffett was named the second wealthiest man in the world. He had long said that he was going to give away the bulk of his money upon his death. But that year he changed his mind. He decided he wouldn't wait until he died. He pledged to gradually give away most of his fortune to five foundations, with the vast majority of it going to the Bill & Melinda Gates Foundation. His giving in 2006 began with his donation of stock shares worth about $1.5 billion to that foundation, along with millions to the other four foundations, which are each operated by one of his children. The total that will eventually go from Buffett's fortune into philanthropic giving is estimated at over $37 billion.

Just two years after making his grand philanthropic venture, Buffett moved up to first position as the richest man in the world, and even with his remarkable ongoing annual contributions, he has remained in the top three each year through the present. Some questioned why Buffet chose to use the Gates Foundation as a conduit to give his money to the people and causes that need it. He explained that he recognized that Bill and Melinda Gates already have staff and structure in place to be able to handle that amount of contribution, and he saw that they personally stay involved and gather data and information to make wise and appropriate decisions regarding the disbursement of the foundation's money.

It's still astounding to me. The two richest men in the world continue to give away billions of dollars to help care for the poor and underprivileged throughout the world, and they still remain among the top three richest men in the world. In the same way, when we choose to care for the poor, God continues to care for us. We simply can't beat God giving. Remember that, my daughter: you can't beat God giving. The more you give to minister to the needs of others, the more God will continue to bless you and meet your needs.

OVERCOMING PSYCHOLOGICAL BARRIERS

What I am telling you is nothing new. Most Christians have heard all this before. But psychological barriers keep many from embracing this knowledge and applying it in their lives. There are psychological barriers that they must overcome in order to act on what they know. These barriers keep them from producing, from planning their purchases, and from recognizing their value. Rather than simply doing those things that will help them get their finances straight, they come up with excuses: "I'm from a broken home," "I went through a bad relationship," "I had to drop out of school," "I had a baby out of wedlock," or "I had my job downsized." There is always an excuse for not doing what God wants them to do.

It's a psychological barrier because they are each living life as a victim. They fail to recognize that they are more than conquerors in Christ Jesus (Romans 8:37). This doesn't mean, however, that they have not been victimized. Some time ago someone did treat them badly, did take advantage of them, and did wound them deeply. But that one experience has now become the focus of their lives. It could have been fifteen years ago that the incident happened, so for fifteen years they have been reliving that experience. Instead of living in the now, they are still imprisoned in that experience of fifteen years ago. Rather than getting help, finding healing, and moving on, they embraced the victim mentality and have been living as victims ever since.

Baby girl, I don't ever want you to live life as a victim. If you do, you will find that men will treat you like a victim. They'll treat you according to the way you act. If you act like you are special, they will treat you like someone special. If you love yourself, men will love you. If you respect yourself, men will respect you. If you take care of yourself, men will take care of you. Don't develop a psychological barrier that keeps you from experiencing relationships the way God intended.

WHEN MEN WON'T CHANGE

Daughter, realize that you cannot make decisions for other adults in your life. Some women think that they can make their husbands change. They even got married with this idea in their minds: "I don't like the way he acts now, and I don't like the way he treats me now; but once we get married, he will be different. I'll change him." Three months into the marriage, the wife comes crying to her pastor, "I don't know what's wrong with my husband. He doesn't act right; he acts like a fool. He doesn't treat me right. And I don't know how to change him." Her husband may be a fool, but she's even a bigger fool for thinking that she can change him and believing that saying "I do" would cause him to be different. He's a grown man. She can't *make* him do anything. She isn't God; she can't change his heart.

I don't do counseling anymore at our church. The church became too big for me to see all those who wanted to come for counseling. God reminded me that He had called me to preach and teach the gospel, and told me that I should leave the counseling to someone who has that calling upon his or her life. Even though I studied psychology and had learned counseling techniques, He told me to be faithful to the calling He has on my life and quit using my time trying to do what somebody else is supposed to be doing. Even though I don't counsel anymore, I do remember some of those counseling sessions.

It wasn't unusual for a woman to come to talk with me about how her marriage wasn't working out. A typical session might go like this: I would explain to the woman that I only had an hour to spend with her, so we needed to get quickly to the heart of the matter. Then I would ask the first of three questions: "What's going on? Tell me what's happening." Her response would often be to spend the first thirty minutes complaining about her husband: "On our wedding day, he said, 'I do,' but he hasn't said it since. Now, it's all 'I don't.'" He says, "'I don't do dishes. I don't do housework. I don't change diapers. I don't take care of the kids. I don't feel like keeping a full-time job. I don't need to go to church. I don't need to keep telling you that I love you. I don't want to stay home all the time; I want to be with *my* friends.'" So she would continue on in that vein for at least thirty minutes or more.

When she finally came up for air, I would ask my second question: "If you had the ideal marriage, what would it look like?" Then she would begin, basically sharing the opposite of each of the things she enumerated as his faults. She would say, for instance, "He would help me do dishes and help around the house. He would help with our children. He would stay employed at a regular job. He would take us to church. He would let me know that he still loves me. He would want to stay home and do things with the kids and me." For twenty minutes, she would continue painting this Norman Rockwell scene of their family the way she envisioned it.

WHAT'S A WOMAN TO DO?

Then I would ask my final question: "What are you going to do?" Most often, she would continue with the same mindset: "Well, he needs to get himself together. He needs to start . . . ." But I would stop her in mid-sentence: "No, I didn't ask what *he* is going to do. I asked what *you* are going to do." She would pause, think for a minute, and then realize that she couldn't base the solution to her situation on something over which she had no control. He was a grown man. He was the only one who could decide what he would or wouldn't do. She wasn't responsible for him and his decisions. She was responsible for herself, her attitudes, her actions, and her decisions. So then she would begin to say things such as, "Well, I'm just not going to live like this anymore. I'm not dumb and worthless, like he tries to make me feel. I can think, I can learn, and I can make a life for my children and me with or without him. I can get a part-time job and finish the degree I was working on when we got married. I love my kids and I can provide for them. It may not be a lot while I'm finishing school, but someday I can give them some of the nicer things we can't have now. And they can learn from me what it means to work hard for those they love and to accomplish something meaningful with their lives." And in those last few minutes of our time together, she would see that God had placed within her all that she needed for all that He had called her to do with her life.

Verse 28 of Proverbs 31 begins, "Her children arise and call her blessed." We don't know from where they are arising. Are they simply standing to honor her? Or does this reflect upon the condition the children were in before their mother decided to make something of her life? If their mother was down in the dumps, the children would have been down there with her. But these children knew their mother deserved praise. They knew she was loving and caring, wise and hard working. They could be proud of her and they praised her.

The second part of verse 28, along with verse 29, reveals that her husband also praises her: ". . . her husband also, and he praises her: 'Many women do noble things, but you surpass them all.'" How could a man *not* praise a woman like this? She was full of action, handling her business, caring for her family, giving to the needy in her community, and preparing for the future. She is a woman worthy of praise.

Daughter, note that this man was a proud husband praising his wife, not a man prostituting a woman. Sadly, some unmarried women allow men to make prostitutes of them. Prostitution isn't always about standing on street corners. It is about selling what should be given in love to someone. A woman who is letting a man sleep with her just because he provides for her financially is living as a prostitute. She is giving herself to a man, and in exchange, he rations out money to her. He never gives her enough to get on her feet herself; he gives her just enough to keep her coming back. He gives her a little for rent, a little for gas, a little for her kids to go to camp and such. Daughter, be sure that you always have your money straight. When you have your own degree, your own job, your own house, your own car, and have a heart to care for others, a man *has* to recognize your qualities.

A Woman Worthy of Praise

There's one last thing I want you to see in this chapter. Verse 31 says, "Honor her for all that her hands have done, and let her works bring her praise at the city gate." This woman didn't get praised only at home, but she got praised at the city gate, that is, she got praise from the community. Some men are foolish enough to believe that they are the only ones praising their women or giving them a compliment. But a woman like this earns praise from all who know her. She has God's favor and the praise of man as well.

This woman is getting so much praise because she deserves such praise. She has been through so much but has come out victoriously. She has competed in a sexist world and made a place for herself. She has learned how to be productive, and she works hard. She looks beyond her own needs, caring for the needs of her family and community as well. As you are doing these things in your own life, baby girl, remember that last verse: "Charm is deceptive, and beauty is fleeting; but a woman who fears the LORD is to be praised."

CHAPTER 5

Handle Your Blessings

Do You

When the queen of Sheba heard about the fame of Solomon and his relationship to the LORD, she came to test Solomon with hard questions. Arriving at Jerusalem with a very great caravan—with camels carrying spices, large quantities of gold, and precious stones—she came to Solomon and talked with him about all that she had on her mind. Solomon answered all her questions; nothing was too hard for the king to explain to her. When the queen of Sheba saw all the wisdom of Solomon and the palace he had built, the food on his table, the seating of his officials, the attending servants in their robes, his cupbearers, and the burnt offerings he made at the temple of the LORD, she was overwhelmed. She said to the king, "The report I heard in my own country about your achievements and your wisdom is true. But I did not believe these things until I came and saw with my own eyes. Indeed, not even half was told me; in wisdom and wealth you have far exceeded the report I heard."

1 KINGS 10:1-7

YOU ARE MORE THAN A BIRD OR A BEE

Daughter, I had planned to talk with you in this chapter about the proverbial birds and bees, but God told me He didn't want me talking to you about the birds *or* the bees. Only a few birds are monogamous; most mate for just one season or less. Female bees will mate with as many male bees as possible. Regarding sex, God wants you to know that you are of a higher order and He expects far more from you than from birds or bees.

The first thing I want you to know, baby girl, is that your desire for a relationship with a man is natural and normal. You were created with that desire as a part of your make-up. It's not only okay for you to feel that way; it's *good* for you to feel that way. That desire comes whether you are even consciously thinking about men or not. The challenging thing is not how to develop an interest in a man, but how to connect with a man who has the qualities you admire, as well as a relationship with God, which will allow you to consider a possible future with him.

Now, there are some people who will say that a woman doesn't have to do anything to connect with a man. In fact, they will say that a Christian woman should just sit at home and wait for God to bring her man along. They quote Proverbs 18:22: "He who finds a wife finds what is good and receives favor from the LORD." This is true. When a man finds a wife, he finds something good. But that does not mean that *only* the man can find something good. The verse could just as easily read, in keeping with Scripture, "When a woman finds a husband, she finds something good." Marriage is not good *only* for the man. If there is a marriage that is good only for the husband, then there is something wrong with that marriage. God does not bring two people together for one of them to be happy and the other to be miserable. A marriage in which only the husband feels that he has found something good is not a marriage in which the man "receives favor from the LORD." Both the husband and the wife should feel that way.

Faith Without Works is Dead

I feel so bad when I think of some woman sitting at home alone night after night just praying for God to bring her a man. That would be the same as an unemployed woman who sits at home day after day just praying for God to bring her a job. It's the same as a woman desperately wanting to be a school teacher who, instead of going to school to get a degree that will allow her to teach, goes home from a dreary job night after night and sits in her room praying for God to make her a teacher.

It's no wonder that so many single women become frustrated, irritable, and hard to get along with. They feel that they can't get angry with God because they are praying to Him for a husband, so they take that anger out on everybody else around them. Instead of getting out and enjoying the company of their peers, becoming women who are living their lives abundantly and meeting potential mates in the process, they sit at home alone, becoming more and more self-absorbed and bitter. They may feel a sense of spiritual superiority over other women who are actually out enjoying life and meeting men, but that sense of spiritual superiority only translates into arrogance, which makes them even less attractive.

"So," you ask, "what should I do then to make a connection with a good man? I'm willing to do something, but I don't know what to do." My advice to you, my daughter, is do *you*. It's not about doing your hair, doing your nails, or doing your makeup. It's about doing the inner you. You need to learn to be the best *you* possible, the *you* God created you to be. In this chapter I want to talk with you about some things that will help you to do *you*.

Baby girl, there is nothing wrong with being honest about your feelings. There is nothing wrong in pursuing a man. At the same time, you need to know that there are some positive ways to pursue a man and some ways you will want to avoid. Now, when I say "pursue" a man, I'm not talking about stalking him! You don't need to find out where he lives and do occasional drive-bys at his home. You don't need to figure out his daily schedule in order to try to encounter him "by accident" every place he goes. Most men are not attracted to women who are too readily available. Those women appear too eager, too desperate, and that is not attractive. It will usually drive a man away, not draw him closer.

Sometimes just the way you look at a man can let him know that you are open to getting to know him better. Eighty to ninety percent of communication is nonverbal. Your eyes and your body speak a language that is clearer sometimes than the words you say. This doesn't mean staring at a man until he feels uncomfortable or batting your eyelids until he thinks something is wrong with you. Learn to smile with your eyes. Someone once said that "the eyes are the window of the soul." Don't be afraid to let what you feel in your soul come out through your eyes.

We see examples in the Bible of God bringing women to men when men were not pursuing them at all. Adam wasn't pursuing Eve. Genesis 2:22 tells us that after God created Eve, "he brought her to the man." Moses was not seeking a wife when he and Zipporah came together. They first met in the wilderness, in the desert. Zipporah and her six sisters were trying to water their father's sheep at a well when some shepherds came along and drove them off. Moses happened to be sitting there, and when he saw what was happening, he got up and rescued the women. Then he went a step further and even watered their flock for them. When the sisters got home, their father Reuel, (also known as Jethro), asked them why they had come in so early. They told him what had happened, so their father sent them to find the man and bring him home. He convinced Moses to stay with them. The Bible doesn't give us details, but it is obvious that a relationship developed between Moses and Zipporah. Moses didn't go out in pursuit of her, but his courageous and compassionate actions of rescuing her and her sisters brought about circumstances that allowed them to meet. From their initial encounter Zipporah knew what sort of man Moses was, and over time Zipporah let Moses get to know what sort of woman she was and, eventually, her father agreed to let them marry.

SEEK A SOUL MATE, NOT A SOLE MATE

In addition to knowing that it is okay for you to show interest in a man, you need to understand, too, Daughter, that there is not just one particular man out there whom you have to find and marry. It is not true that out of approximately seven billion people in the world, God has only one man chosen for you. You do not need to wait for God to somehow mysteriously navigate the circumstances of life and, no matter where he was born or where you were born, bring the two of you together. Baby girl, more than one woman has been chasing the same man for twenty years because she thinks, "He's the one. I know that God wants us to be together. He may not be interested in me yet, but I know he will be because I'm sure this is the man that God has for me. And what God has for me is for me!"

Baby, there are millions of men out there. You don't have to keep waiting for, or chasing after, some man who doesn't want you. If he doesn't want you, you don't want him either. Open your eyes. Look around. Don't look for that one man; look for a *type* of man. Look for a man who has received Jesus as his Savior, a man filled with the Spirit of God, a man who loves God and seeks to please Him with his life, a man with a job and goals for the future, a man of character who has a loving heart. That doesn't describe just one man. There are many men who will someday become good, loving husbands. You don't need to find one particular man among all the men alive on earth today; you just need to find one of *those* men.

Being in the will of God may lead you to a soul mate, but you are not looking for a sole man—the one and only man who is ordained by God to be your husband. Being in the will of God means keeping in step with Him; letting Him be involved in your desire to find a husband; letting Him guide you in all aspects of your life; evaluating the men you meet by His standards, not by the man's looks, his checkbook, or how he makes you feel; and looking for God's nod of approval when you find a man with whom you would like to spend the rest of your life.

It isn't easy for a woman to find a good man today. I admit that. The statistics are working against you. In the first place, there are more women in the world than men. Also, millions of men are in prison right now. In addition, thousands of men have been married three or four times. If he has already messed up that many times, you don't want to be next in line for one of his failed marriages. There are also the drug addicts and alcoholics. And you certainly don't want the boy who will never grow up and accept responsibility, keep a job, and be a good father to your children. So the odds are against a woman finding a good man. But there are still good men out there! Don't let the statistics discourage you. You only need one good man, not millions of them. And there are men out there who love God and are just as eager to find a Proverbs 31 wife as you are to find a Moses. You just need to be sure you are looking for the right sort of person.

FINDING MR. RIGHT

It is more important to focus on *who* he is than *where* he is. Rather than roaming around trying to find a place where you might meet a good man, keep a mental image of the man you want that includes his character, his attributes, his values, his relationship with God, and all of those things that are important to you when you think about "till death do us part." That way, when you meet that type of man—no matter where he is—you will recognize him.

Also, ask yourself if you are mature enough to handle a permanent relationship. Are you ready to settle down for the rest of your life with one man? Have you developed within you the qualities of a Proverbs 31 woman? Those are the things that a "good man" will be looking for. Will he find those things in you? If you find a mature Christian man to whom you are attracted but he sees you as a self-centered, immature woman, it doesn't matter how much *you* like *him*. A good man is looking for a good woman.

Recently I read that the number-one place where people connect in relationships is at work. Church, of course, is a good place to meet a good man. School is another. If you are an intelligent woman attending school to prepare yourself to do something meaningful with your life, you are going to want a man who is doing, or has done, the same thing. You may meet someone quite naturally in your neighborhood or while working together on a project in your community. Then, of course, your girlfriends may want to set you up.

Of course, a whole new craze is happening in this computerized twenty-first century world. Now men and women go online to find a relationship. People often ask me what I think about online dating. Before I give my answer, I must acknowledge that I'm old. I know I'm old; I'm in my 40s. I'm so old that I remember rotary telephones. To call someone, we put an index finger in the correct numbered circle on the dial, moved the dial around until it hit a silver piece of metal, pulled our finger out and waited for the dial to go back to the starting point. Then we would repeat the process for the next number and the next until we had dialed the entire number. I'm old.

But I have to tell you, online dating doesn't make sense to me. That doesn't make it wrong just because it doesn't make sense to me. It is simply another avenue by which two people might connect. People who oppose online dating will argue that the person you meet could be lying; he could be misrepresenting himself. Well, the man you met at work could also be lying to you and misrepresenting himself. Those same people say that you could meet someone online who says he's single when he's actually married. Well, if truth be told, you could meet some man in a singles' group at church who you later find out is married. Not everyone who attends church is a Christian, so it isn't just people online who are misrepresenting themselves. Therefore, I'm not saying a woman shouldn't go online to try to meet a good man. But what I am saying is that no matter where she meets him, she still needs to become friends with him first.

MEETING IS JUST THE FIRST STEP

Meeting someone to whom you are attracted is just the first step. Then you have to really get to know each other and become friends. In that process you will find out how he lives his life, how he relates to his family, and how he approaches his job. You will also discover what he believes about God and what values and moral standards he holds, as well as his plans and dreams for the future. This is all part of the dating process.

But there is one thing to keep in mind, Daughter. Your man will go back to the place you first met him. My wife Sharon was never surprised to see me in church time and time again because that is where we met. If you meet a man at work, you know he's going to go back to work. If you meet him at school, you know he's going to keep going back there for his classes. And if you meet a man online, be assured that he will be going back online. The issue is that you don't know his online habits. He *will* be online, but what websites does he frequent? Does he hang out in chat rooms? How much time does he spend online? Is his computer a tool that he uses or is it an addiction?

There is one other thing I must make clear when I say that an online dating service is a possible means for meeting a man (not one I would recommend, but one that is plausible). I am only talking about adults. Young girls and teenagers have no business meeting people online. There are too many pedophiles, or sexual predators, roaming online seeking whom they may devour. Cyberspace is a dangerous place for young people to visit. Parents need to protect their children online just as much as they do in other places. Some parents who are so careful to monitor where their children go and who they are with are either naïve or simply foolish for not monitoring their use of a computer with as much intensity. Every parent needs to know their children's passwords, to go on Facebook and see with whom they are connecting, and to use safeguards on their computers that provide boundaries for their children's netsurfing.

Now let's back up and talk about the importance of being the best you possible. If you want to find a good man, you need to be sure that you are a good woman. If you want a man of substance, then you are going to have to be a woman of substance. When the queen of Sheba set out in pursuit of King Solomon, he was not wondering about her. He was not seeking her; instead, she sought him out. She knew, however, that she could probably have a relationship with him because they were equals. He was a king, but she was a queen. He had great wealth, but she had money, too. He was a very wise man, but she was intelligent also. He was a leader, but she was a leader as well.

Baby girl, you can't go after a man with kingly potential if you aren't developing your own queenly potential. You can't go after a man who has everything if you've got nothing. You have to bring something to the table. Daughter, you are very special. When you go out of my home, keep in mind who you are. You are a priceless original; don't come back as a cheap copy of somebody else. You are a woman of purpose; don't come back confused about who you are. You are a woman who serves Christ; don't come back with your allegiance belonging to someone else. You are a woman of destiny; don't come back duped. Don't become so desperate for a man that you forget who you are, and let him think for you, use you, and abuse you. Always be mindful of who you are and Whose you are.

Don't Leave Them Behind

There's another lesson you can learn from the queen of Sheba. Make sure you take your support system with you. First Kings 10:2 says that she arrived at Jerusalem, "with a very great caravan." She went to find King Solomon, but she didn't go by herself; she had a large group of attendants traveling with her. She had her support system with her—not only on the trip there, but on the trip back as well. She needed her support group for protection. It would not have been safe for her to travel by herself from Africa to Israel. As a single woman traveling alone, she would have been vulnerable to anyone who wanted to attack her, rob her, hurt her, or even kill her.

Daughter, don't try to travel through life by yourself. Take your support system with you for security. God has blessed you with a wonderful support system. You have a church that supports your relationship with Jesus, teaches you to rely on the power of the Holy Spirit in your life, encourages you to use the spiritual gifts you have been given, and helps you to pursue holiness in your daily life. You have parents who love you, pray for you, and have brought you up in the ways of the Lord. You have Christian friends who love you, encourage you, and help you keep your life on track by holding you accountable for your actions. They aren't going to let you act like a fool without calling you on it: "Girl, you know we aren't supposed to act like that." God has blessed you with a loving and faithful support system, and you need those voices in your life.

There are some brothers who are so messed up that they will try to separate you from your support system. Don't let that happen. If you connect with such a man, he will try to convince you that the other voices in your life are wrong and only his is right. He will discourage you from going to church, from hanging out with your friends, and even from talking with your own parents. He is smooth. He will sweet talk you and make you feel that you are special in his life. He will try to get you to the point that you believe him, are emotionally attached to him, and depend upon him for everything. Once you are entrenched in that mindset, then he can control you. At first you may think he just loves you so much that he's jealous, and you feel flattered. You don't realize that he is mentally sick and his goal is to dominate you. Whenever you enter a relationship with a man, continue to keep your support group close. Listen to them. Trust their voices. If they have been guiding you lovingly and faithfully all these years, you can count on them to tell you the truth. You can trust them to be objective observers who continue to influence you in positive ways. If a man can't accept you *with* your support system, he is not the one for you.

TAKE YOUR TIME

There's one thing I want to mention to you here, my daughter. As we look at the story of the queen of Sheba, we see that she was going to Solomon simply to meet him, not to marry him. Don't think that every man you meet is the man you are going to marry. That's a quick way to scare a man off.

Let's say your girlfriend hooks you up with a nice guy. You meet him for coffee, think he's a great person, and your mind starts wandering: "He's the one. I just know it. Look how God works. He's wonderful. We're going to be so happy together. . . ." This poor guy is asking you to pass the sugar, and you're already waiting for him to ask you to marry him. Because you've built up this whole scenario in your mind, you also begin to build great expectations as well. This man simply came to meet you and have coffee, but you get angry because he doesn't call you the next day. If he does call to ask you for a casual date, you take it as a confirmation that you are to be together. He's thinking dinner and a movie. You're thinking wedding bells.

The problem isn't with him, but with you. You don't even know who he is below the surface. You know the way he presents himself, but you don't yet know what really matters to him. You may know he's a Christian, but what is his relationship with Jesus really like? Does he let God direct his life, or does he just go to church on Sunday? He may own a Bible that he carries with him to church on Sunday, but does he ever open it on any other day? You may know that he has a good job and makes a lot of money, but on what does he spend his money? Does he tithe, give money to the poor, and invest in his future? Or is he like a little child, spending every penny he makes on games, toys, clothes, and entertainment? You don't know this man, but in your mind, you are already planning to marry him.

Within two weeks you start treating him like a husband even though he's only seeing you as a friend. Why does he see you that way? Because that's all you are. But you are already seeing yourself as his wife, so you start behaving accordingly. You invite him over for dinner every evening. He talks about how busy he is, so you offer to do his laundry. When you go to his place, you wash his dishes and clean his house. And because you are thinking of yourself as his wife, you begin to rationalize that it really would be okay for you to have sex with him. Since the two of you are headed for marriage, you reason that it wouldn't really be a sin—just a premature consummation of that relationship into which God is bringing you. The most unhealthy thoughts can sound so rational when we are in love— or in lust.

When I went to Dallas for the 2011 Super Bowl, the entire country was being hit by sleet, snow, and ice. Even in places where it rarely ever snowed, it was snowing. Indianapolis was certainly not exempt. The weather here was terrible. Two days before I was supposed to leave, the Indianapolis International Airport delayed and even cancelled many, many flights. Of course, during this time I was praying for the Lord to clear up the weather so that I could get to the Super Bowl. God heard my prayers. On the day I was supposed to leave, everything cleared up. The sun was shining. It was cold, but there was no snow, sleet, or rain. I felt great. When I got to the airport, I couldn't believe it when the flight departure screen showed that the flight was on time. We boarded the plane. I got my seatbelt on. We were pulling back from the gate. Then the pilot came on the sound system and said our take-off was going to be delayed because he had run out of deicing fluid. He said, too, that it would take some time.

One hour passed. Two hours passed. We were getting anxious. The pilot came back on the sound system again and asked us to be patient. He explained that the rest of the plane was fine now, but they were having a problem deicing the tail. He told us that we couldn't take off if the tail wasn't right because, if the tail weren't right, we couldn't get to our destination—we would crash. So, for our own safety, they were delaying the take-off to take care of this tail problem. Even as he was speaking, God spoke to me and told me that's what He wanted me to tell His daughters: "The reason I have delayed your take off and won't let you get to your destination is because you have not dealt properly with your tail. If you don't have it covered properly, once you take off you will crash and get hurt, and you won't make it to your destination. But if you let the Holy Spirit do His work in you first, you will be able to get to where you're supposed to be." Handle yourself first!

WHAT DO YOU KNOW ABOUT HIM?

The queen of Sheba teaches us something here. She had heard about Solomon's name and fame and how he honored the name of God. Why was she interested in him? Because she had heard of his attributes and his relationship with God. She wasn't interested because of how he looked, but because of what he was about. When you have an opportunity to meet a man, you first need to check out his name. The Bible says a good name, or reputation, is better than gold. (See Proverbs 22:1.) As recorded in Acts 6:3, when the apostles sought out men to serve as deacons in the church, they said to the leaders, "Brothers and sisters, choose seven men from among you who are known to be full of the Spirit and wisdom." They were looking for men "who are known to be . . ."—men with a good reputation for being full of the Spirit and wisdom.

Daughter, if you were interested in a particular man, my question to you would be this: what have you heard about him? I'm not talking about what he typed to you online because that's just him talking about himself. What do his friends say about him? What does his family say about him? What do his coworkers say about him? What do other women say about him? What do people at his church say about him? What does his momma say about him? (If his mother doesn't say something good about him, there's nothing good about him to say. She knows the man.) What have you heard? If you haven't heard anything about him, don't connect with him yet. Wait until you get a fuller picture of him and know whether or not he has "a good name."

The queen of Sheba had heard so many good things about Solomon. She heard about his fame (which would have included his wisdom, power, wealth, etc.) and his relationship with the Lord. What she heard about him was so good, she didn't really believe it. She decided she had to go see for herself. She was a smart woman. She learned about Solomon from what others shared, but she didn't form an opinion of her own until she met the man for herself. In your case, Daughter, you may have heard that your man is a Christian. Have you seen any signs of Christianity in his life? You've heard that he loves his children. Have you seen him relate to any children? Have you seen any nurturing qualities? How does he get along with them? You've heard that he's a part of the church. Have you seen his involvement first hand? Have you seen him give his time, talents, and money to support what God is doing through his church? You heard he has a job. Have you seen any evidence that he has that job? You know the things he has told you. Are his actions, his speech, and his lifestyle backing up what he has said?

When we go to get our first driver's license, we may want it so much. We may have studied the manual and memorized the material until we get a perfect score on the written test. But even though we've gone to all that trouble, the Bureau of Motor Vehicles still doesn't give us a license yet. They then insist that we get in a car and actually demonstrate that we can apply what we know by our driving. It's not enough to know something in our heads; we have to actually demonstrate that knowledge, and apply it with wisdom. In the same way, you can't evaluate the character of a man simply by what you hear from others or what he *says*. You have to see those things demonstrated in his life.

ASK THE HARD QUESTIONS

It was Solomon's wisdom that drew the queen of Sheba to him. She wouldn't have taken her "hard questions" to any lesser man because she was an intelligent woman herself. She wouldn't have gone to a man her equal with hard questions; she would have known as much as he did. But she heard that this man Solomon possessed greater wisdom than anyone else on earth. Note that it wasn't his *knowledge* she sought, but his *wisdom*. There is a difference. Knowledge is about the information one has in his or her mind. It's about having a grasp of facts and ideas. Wisdom involves good judgment, good sense, insight, the ability to make good decisions, and the ability to apply knowledge. It was Solomon's wisdom that attracted the queen.

Baby girl, don't be afraid to ask hard questions of your man. If he is like Solomon, he will be open to your questions and will answer them honestly and directly. If you ever catch him in a lie or trying to shade the truth a bit, you must realize that you can never have a good relationship with him. You cannot get close to somebody who lies to you. You cannot have intimacy with someone without honesty. That's why the hard questions must come at the beginning of a relationship. You don't wait until two weeks before the wedding and then ply him with questions. This isn't a final exam you're conducting; it's an entrance exam. You need to know if you want to enter into a relationship with this man. If he cannot pass the entrance exam, he won't be able to handle the relationship.

When you are doing your evaluation, don't grade him on a curve. Don't say, "Well, he's got problems, but he's better than my girlfriend's husband." No, baby girl. Keep your standards high and ask the *hard* questions. You don't have to ask them all at once. You're not interrogating a criminal; you're finding out if this could be the man of your dreams. But as you are getting to know him, and before your relationship gets serious, the questions should come out naturally in the course of conversations with him. What do I mean by hard questions? Here are some examples:

What does Jesus mean to you?

To what church do you belong, and what is your involvement there?

Are you married? Are you in a relationship right now?

Have you been married before? If yes, how many times?

When was your last serious relationship?

What did you do that helped bring about the demise of that marriage/relationship?

Do you have any children? If yes, what are your custody arrangements? Do you pay your child support? How do you maintain relationship with your children?

Do you live with anyone right now?

Don't be afraid to ask the hard questions. When you're married, the questions don't get any easier. If a man isn't willing to answer your questions now, he certainly won't answer any questions once you are married. If he is hiding anything from you now, a marriage to this man would be built on a very shaky foundation. As he responds to your questions, you will not only learn facts about your man, but you will be able to assess his wisdom as well. Does he show good judgment? Has he made a series of bad decisions? Is he wise in the way he handles his relationships? What are the priorities that are showing up? Can you take confidence in his wisdom?

MONEY MATTERS

The queen of Sheba not only learned about Solomon's wisdom, but also about his resources. She not only heard about all of his wealth and possessions, but she also saw them with her own eyes. In 1 Kings 10:7, she says to Solomon: "But I did not believe these things until I came and saw with my own eyes. Indeed, not even half was told me; in wisdom and wealth you have far exceeded the report I heard." It was not only his wisdom that exceeded his reputation, but his wealth as well. How about your man? How does he handle his resources? Why is it important that your man knows how to manage resources? The number one reason for divorce in America is money. It is not adultery; it's not unfaithfulness. It's money.

Of course, when you're in a new relationship, you think, "Money doesn't matter to us. We love each other. We don't really care about material things. Our love will see us through." Daughter, you need to understand now that money *does* matter. Love can't pay a mortgage, buy a car, or put food on the table. You are going to need money for those things. And it isn't only about whether or not you have money. Divorces aren't usually the result of not having any money, but rather not being able to agree on how to manage the money the couple does have.

When we read 1 Kings 9:25, we find that King Solomon had built an altar for the Lord where he regularly brought offerings. This came after the previous chapter, which tells us that Solomon had finished the construction of a temple for the Lord. At the consecration of that temple, he brought such a great offering to the Lord that it couldn't fit on the altar. Does your man give to God liberally, or does he skimp on what he gives the Lord? Does God get his first fruits or his leftovers? Does he tithe to God or just tip Him? If a man doesn't love God enough to give to Him, why do you think he will love you enough to give to you? You didn't create him, die on the cross for him, see him through one difficulty after another, promise him an abundant life, or bless him materially and spiritually. How he gives to the One who gave him everything is very significant.

When a man gives to God, it speaks of his obedience because God commands us to give. When a man gives to God, it speaks of his affection towards God "for where your treasure is, there your heart will be also" (Matthew 6:21). When a man gives to God, it speaks of his faith because he trusts that if he gives as God asks, God will keep his promise to "open the floodgates of heaven and pour out so much blessing that there will not be room enough to store it" (Malachi 3:10). If a man obeys, loves, and trusts God, he is far more likely to honor, love, and trust others as well.

A man's willingness to give to God also means that he is more likely to be willing to give to others. The queen of Sheba was overwhelmed by how much Solomon accomplished. The building of the temple, the administration of the government, the formation of an army, and the hundreds of projects Solomon initiated created countless jobs for the people. Solomon realized that when God blessed him, it wasn't just for him. He knew that he was expected to turn around and bless somebody else. The queen even experienced Solomon's generosity in a personal way. When she came to meet Solomon, she brought spices, gold, and precious gems to him. When it was time for her to return home, he gave to her in such great abundance that she took home more than she had brought with her. Theirs was a reciprocal relationship. She gave to him, but he gave to her as well. Likewise, if a man loves you, my daughter, he will give to you even as you are giving to him. If you are doing all of the giving, he doesn't love you—no matter what words may be coming from his lips. If he truly loves you, he will give to you. A person can give without loving, but a person can't love without giving.

I was in Atlanta, Georgia, preaching at Ray of Hope Church, where Dr. Cynthia Hale is the pastor. She's a great preacher and a great person too. One evening after a service, I went to a restaurant to eat and catch a late NBA game. There was a couple sitting right next to me. As they were getting ready to leave, the man reached into his pocket, took out a couple dollars, and tossed them on the table as a tip. The woman looked over at him and said, "You can't be my man tipping like that." He responded by dipping back into his pocket and bringing out some more money. This woman was making it clear that she doesn't want a man who doesn't know how to tip because that says something is wrong either with his head or with his heart. If he can't calculate 18 or 20 percent of the bill in his head, it's a head issue. If it doesn't matter to him that his server, who had been caring for his needs all evening, depends on tips to make a living wage, then it's a heart issue. Either way, this woman realized that the way this man tipped revealed something about him that she needed to address. What a man gives to God, gives to others, and gives to you says a lot about who he is.

God Didn't Rest Till the Seventh Day

There is one point I want to make clear about finances and about finding a man who has a good work ethic. Baby girl, you do not want to connect with a man who doesn't have a work ethic. This means something different from simply having a job. There are some men who are hardworking, but in today's economy, with the unemployment rate so high, it is really hard for them to find a good job—a job commensurate with their ability. I'm sure you know at least one man who is unemployed but still works. He's always doing something—always finding a small job here or there to do, always volunteering to help others, always doing things to care for his family, always offering his services at the church, always doing something positive. That's because he has a strong work ethic. He isn't lazy and doesn't just sit around, waiting for someone to take care of him.

Then, too, I'm sure you know at least one man who has a job but won't work. He does as little as possible on his job. He is not even ashamed if coworkers have to do more than their

share of the work to make up for what he isn't doing. He's lazy
when he gets home, too. He lets his wife do all of the housework,
provide all the care for the children, do the grocery shopping
and the laundry, and then expects her to meet all of his needs
and desires in bed as well. It's no wonder that he has energy and
she doesn't! He has no work ethic, and he certainly has no right
to talk about loving the woman he is using and abusing.

David Page, senior pastor of New Baptist Church in
Indianapolis, and I went out to eat one day. I parked in a metered
space right in front of the restaurant. Before I could get out
some change, Pastor Page had already jumped out of the car and
was putting money into the meter. He seemed to be putting in an
excessive number of coins, so I said to him, "We aren't going to
stay in here that long." He replied, "No, Pastor. I didn't know that
the meter was broken until I started putting money in. It just
keeps taking the coins." I said, "Wait a minute. You put money in
it at first because you didn't know it was broken. But after you
found out that it was broken, why did you keep putting money in
it?"

I would ask you the same thing, Daughter, if you were to
keep investing in a man who doesn't work. Because he looks like
he works, you might not have realized that he was out of order at
first. But once you realized that you were putting more and more
in and getting nothing in return, I would question your behavior.
If a man doesn't work, there is something wrong with him. You
need to move on. Don't let him take all that you have and leave
you wanting.

Don't Believe the Fairy Tale

First Kings 10:10 says, "Never again were so many spices
brought in as those the queen of Sheba gave to King Solomon."

It's interesting to me that even though the queen brought gold and jewels for the king, the story focuses more on the spices. Let me take some liberty with this attention given to the spices and do a little play on words. I would encourage you, Daughter, not to give away your "spices" before you meet your king. Those spices were of great value. The queen could have sold the spices and received a lot of money in return. She also could have given them away to other men along the way just for fun. Probably most of the members of her entourage were men. They would have enjoyed some of her spices and would have felt honored to receive them. But she didn't sell them or give them to anyone but the king. There would be a lot of happier marriages today if the wives had saved their spices for their husbands. Too many women use up all their spices along the way to meeting their king, so they have nothing left then with which to "spice up" their marriage.

There is just one last point I want to reiterate to you about this topic: if a man doesn't have kingly potential before you marry him, he isn't going to have kingly potential after you marry him. If he's not a prince before you marry him, he isn't going to become a prince after you marry him. One of my favorite movies is "The Princess and the Frog." I love that movie. After sixty years, the Disney Company finally has its first Black princess. And Tiana portrays a real sister, too. She talks like a sister, moves like a sister, and has the attitude of a sister. I love that. She is a princess with dreams, visions, and hope. She can cook, but she doesn't want just to cook: she wants to own her own upscale restaurant and to operate her own business. She is pursuing her destination, her dream.

Some people try to hook Tiana up with men, but she declines. She wasn't seeking a man; she was trying to get her own life together for herself. At this point, she runs into a frog. This is where Disney gets it wrong. (Disney has been getting this wrong for sixty years!) Disney has been telling our daughters that if you come across a frog and kiss it, that frog is going to become their handsome prince, and they are going to get married and live happily ever after. This isn't true! If you kiss a frog, it's going to still be a frog! Don't let anyone make you think that you can make something into what you want it to be just by kissing it. Some women actually believe that fairy tale. They go around kissing one frog after another in search of their prince, but all they get is disappointment and disillusionment. Baby, if he isn't a prince before you kiss him, he's not going to be a prince after you kiss him.

About five or six years ago, a certain television commercial showed a woman as a princess. She had on a ball gown, wore a crown and had a scepter in her hand. In her other hand, she held a frog. Like the fairy tale, she thought if she kissed the frog, it would become a prince. So she kissed it. But it didn't become a prince; it became a weasel. She tried again, kissing the weasel. It didn't become a prince, but a buzzard. She kissed the buzzard, yet the buzzard didn't become a prince. It became a skunk instead. She kissed the skunk, and the skunk became a monkey. She kissed the monkey, and the monkey became a half-man/half-jackass. She was so frustrated that she ran away. The half-man/half-jackass called to her, "Wait! Wait! One more kiss! I might be your prince!"

Daughter, how many frogs are you going to kiss? How many weasels, buzzards, skunks, and monkeys are you going to embrace? How many half-men/half-jackasses are you going to believe before you realize that if they aren't your prince before you kiss them, they aren't going to turn into a prince after you kiss them? You've got to work on yourself and your queenly potential. You want to pursue a man who has kingly potential, but you have to bring something to the relationship. It starts with you and your relationship with God. Do you, baby girl. A real king isn't going to be fooled by a female frog trying to look like a princess.

CHAPTER 6

Handle Your Basics

Put a Ring on It

At that time the kingdom of heaven will be like ten virgins who took their lamps and went out to meet the bridegroom. Five of them were foolish and five were wise. The foolish ones took their lamps but did not take any oil with them. The wise ones, however, took oil in jars along with their lamps. The bridegroom was a long time in coming, and they all became drowsy and fell asleep.

At midnight the cry rang out: 'Here's the bridegroom! Come out to meet him!'

Then all the virgins woke up and trimmed their lamps. The foolish ones said to the wise, 'Give us some of your oil; our lamps are going out.'

'No,' they replied, 'there may not be enough for both us and you. Instead, go to those who sell oil and buy some for yourselves.'

But while they were on their way to buy the oil, the bridegroom arrived. The virgins who were ready went in with him to the wedding banquet. And the door was shut.

Later the others also came. 'Lord, Lord,' they said, 'open the door for us!' But he replied, 'Truly I tell you, I don't know you.'

Therefore keep watch, because you do not know the day or the hour.

MATTHEW 25:1-13

THE BRIDEGROOM IS COMING!

In this final chapter of our time together, I want to focus on this topic: put a ring on it. In Matthew 25, Jesus is trying to get His disciples of the first century, and those of the twenty-first century, to understand the kingdom of God—the rule, the reign, and the righteousness of God. In order to help us understand the kingdom of God, he uses this illustration of a wedding ceremony. In the first century, weddings within the Jewish culture were different from ours today. The bride and her friends would wait at the bride's house for the groom to show up. For the bride and the bridesmaids, it was often a weeklong celebration.

The groom was staying at another location with his friends, and the bride didn't know which day he would show up. When the groom decided it was time, he would lead his friends to the house where the bride was, and one of the groomsmen would walk ahead of the groom and shout, "The bridegroom is coming!" Then the bridesmaids would come out of the house with their lamps, and they would go meet the groom. When they met him with their lamps, they would light the way, leading him to his wife for the marriage ceremony. Only those bridesmaids whose lights were shining brightly were supposed to be in the street with the groom. The bride didn't know the day or the hour when her groom might come. He could come at noon, in the evening, or at the midnight hour. Since she and her bridesmaids didn't know when he was coming, they had to stay ready.

Jesus died on the cross for us, God raised Him from the dead, and He sits now at the right hand of the Father. But Jesus also wanted us to know that He is coming again. In this illustration, the church is the bride and Jesus is the Bridegroom. He's coming back to get us, but we don't know which day or what hour He is coming. We who have received Him as Savior and Lord make up the bride of Christ, and we have to stay ready. That's what this text is saying to us.

A Revelation and A Reminder

Naturally, in twenty-first century America our culture is different, and so are our wedding ceremonies. A lamp is no longer important, but a ring is. During the ceremony rings are exchanged between the bride and groom. The wedding ring is symbolic of the love that the groom and bride have for each other. This tradition came from ancient Egypt more than forty-eight hundred years ago. The ring was made of precious metal in the form of a never-ending circle, even as the love between husband and the wife is meant to be special and never ending. The Egyptians chose to put the ring on the third finger of the left hand because they believed a vein ran directly from the third finger straight to the heart. It's a precious thought that the ring is connected directly to the heart and symbolizes the love that is there.

The wedding ring is both a revelation and a reminder. When a woman is wearing a wedding ring, it's a revelation to every man she meets that she is married. It doesn't matter if the man she meets doesn't even know her, her husband, or her family. The ring clearly signifies that she is married. It reveals to all who see it that she has a lifelong commitment to one particular man. It says to those who might be interested that she is unavailable. It's a revelation to those who see it.

The ring is also a reminder. The tradition of men wearing wedding rings is relatively new. During World War II when soldiers went off to battle, they had long separations from their wives. Those husbands wanted something to remind them that they were loved and there was a woman waiting for them to come home. The ring served as a tangible reminder.

My wedding ring certainly serves that dual purpose for me. When I travel around the country, my ring is a revelation to everyone who sees me that I am married. People don't even have to ask me my marital status or wonder if I am available. They can take one glance at my left hand and they know that I am married. The ring also serves as a reminder for me anytime I might be tempted. When I look at it, I remember that I have a loving wife, and I am not about to do anything to hurt her or to damage our relationship. The ring is significant because it is a symbol of commitment at the highest level of relationship. That's why Beyoncé sings, "If you love it, then you ought to put a ring on it."

Daughter, there may be a time when you will meet a man who wants you to give him sex, but he doesn't want to give you a ring. You need to make up your mind before that ever happens that until he gives you a ring, you'll not be giving him your body. If you wait until you are in the moment and your hormones and emotions are all stimulated, you won't be able to make an objective decision. So make it clear all along the way that sex is meaningful to you. It isn't something you give a man in exchange for dinner and a movie. Your body is the temple of the Holy Spirit, not a brothel. Sex is fun, ecstatic, relaxing, and totally pleasurable, but it is also sacred. The relationship between a husband and wife symbolizes the relationship between Christ and the church, His bride. Therefore, your mindset always needs to be this: until a man puts a wedding ring on your finger, you aren't putting any sexual moves on him.

YOUR FATHER'S BLESSING

Another wedding tradition in our culture is that of the father giving his daughter away. As a minister, I've officiated at hundreds of weddings. At most of them, the bride wanted me to ask the question: "Who gives this woman to be married to this man?" Then the father or father figure would stand up and respond, "I do," or "Her mother and I do." That declaration served as the father's blessing his stamp of approval on the marriage. In essence he was saying that of all the men he knew his daughter could have married, he believed this man would be the best husband to her, so he was giving his endorsement.

When I wanted to marry Sharon over twenty-five years ago, we didn't elope or simply announce our engagement. I had enough respect for her and her father to talk with him before we became engaged. I said to him, "Mr. Henry, Sharon and I have been dating for more than a year and a half now, and we are serious about this relationship. We want to take it to the next level, and I want to ask your daughter to marry me, but I don't want to do it without your approval. I want your blessing on this marriage. So I'm here today asking for your stamp of approval, for your blessing on me marrying your daughter."

Now, Mr. Henry didn't respond, "Okay, Jeffrey, go ahead. You've got my blessing." Instead, he said, "Let's talk about your job a little bit." He asked, "How's work going for you? Is there any security and stability? Do you make enough money to pay for housing so that my daughter can have somewhere to live?" After I responded to those questions, he started talking to me about benefits, insurance, and retirement. "Will my baby be covered by that insurance that you have? How much savings do you have? What are you doing for retirement?" Before he would give his approval to our engagement, he wanted to know that I could take care of his daughter.

Since I've begun this dialogue with you, my daughter, I've started asking myself under what circumstances I would be willing to give my blessing for you to be married. As long as you live in my primary family, I know that you are loved, cared for, and protected. Before I would be willing to release you, I would want to make sure that you are going into another stable situation. That entails more than just having your physical needs met. You are a spiritual, intellectual, and emotional being as well. I would want to know that you would be entering an environment that promotes your well-being in all of these areas.

Whether you were leaving home to be married, or, simply transitioning into life as a single adult woman on your own, there are certain conditions that would have to be met before I would approve. One thing specifically that comes to mind is that you would need to have a place to go. Whether it's moving into marriage or moving out on your own, you would have to have a home. You can't live in inadequate housing or in a place where I would fear for your safety.

Not only that, but I would also need to know that you can take care of yourself. I don't ever want you to develop the mindset that you have to have a man to take care of you. You need to know that your dependency is on the Lord, not on any man. You need to know that no matter what happens to the man in your life, you will not only survive but thrive. The oil in the Matthew 25 passage represents God's Holy Spirit. Daughter, when God redeemed you by the blood of Jesus, He didn't just save you, but He also took up residence within you in the Person of His Holy Spirit. The Holy Spirit equips, enables, and empowers you so that you can take care of yourself.

Oil has a multiplicity of uses. You can use it to light lamps or provide heat. You can cook with oil. Oil can be used to sanctify and set apart. That oil, my daughter, can enable you to recognize that you need not depend upon anybody but the One who supplies the oil in your life. If you are hungry, you can cook. If you are in the dark, you can let your light shine in that situation. If you are cold, you have warmth. If you are sinful, the oil can sanctify you. Before I can release you, I must know that you can take care of yourself.

CHOOSE YOUR FRIENDS WISELY

Another provision of my releasing you is that you must be making friends with the right kind of women. Remember that there were ten virgins: five were foolish, five were wise. If you were to hang out with the foolish crowd, I couldn't let you go because you would undoubtedly make a fool of yourself. When you look at the Scripture passage, you notice that the five foolish virgins are hanging out together, while the five wise virgins are together in a separate group. Wise people and foolish people don't mix. They don't think alike. They don't enjoy one another's company. You have to therefore choose to spend your time with people who are wise.

Remember, Psalm 14:1 says, "The fool says in his heart, 'There is no God.'" You've got to hang out with people wiser than that. You need to be with people who have integrity and purity about them. They need to understand accountability and practice holding one another to a Christian mindset and behavior. You know that association brings about assimilation. Or as Grandma says, "If you lie down with dogs, you're going to get up with fleas." Dr. Lance Watson cautions people about "having a Smartphone, but talking to foolish people about stupid things." That's the same thing as having a Smart Car but riding with foolish people going to crazy places. Until you are surrounding yourself with wise people, I wouldn't be able to release you.

I also need to know that you understand economics and that

you can handle this economy. Those five foolish virgins took just enough oil that they thought they could make it. Why? Because fools always take just enough. They somehow think that "just enough" is going to get it done. There's somebody who did just enough to graduate from junior high school, just enough to graduate from high school, just enough to get a job, and still does just enough to keep that job. And now, she has just enough to make ends meet. Baby girl, that's no way to go through life. There's a huge, wonderful world out there, and I want you to experience it to the fullest. I want you to dream big dreams and do what it takes to make them come true. Don't get trapped in that "just enough" mentality.

The wise virgins didn't take as little as possible. They took extra oil with them. They were prepared because they didn't know just when the bridegroom was coming, and they wanted to be sure that they had enough. They were thinking ahead. They were *wise*. Now, when the foolish virgins ran out of oil, they went to wise virgins and asked for some of their oil. But the wise virgins refused. They weren't being mean or stingy. They were just being wise. They knew that if they shared what oil they had with the others who had let theirs run out, they would run out, too. Then there would be no one there with lamps to go out to meet the bridegroom when he came. They weren't going to leave him wandering around in the darkness with no one responding to the cries, "Here's the bridegroom! Come out and meet him!"

So, rather than disappoint the bridegroom, they told the foolish virgins to go to the store and buy some more oil for themselves. But before those foolish women got back from the store, the bridegroom came and they missed out on the wedding banquet. Daughter, if you go through life with the "just enough" philosophy, you will miss out on one opportunity after another. I won't release you to go out on your own until you show me that you understand economics, can manage money, and that you will not try to live off the labor of others.

ALWAYS BE READY

There is something else I want you to consider from this story in Matthew. Think about the fact that you don't know when your bridegroom is coming. You don't know the day or the hour you will meet your husband. Anytime you leave home, you could possibly be on your way to meet him. Sure, some "foolish virgins" *think* they know. They are sure that they are going to meet their future mate at church, or they are confident that he will be in one of their classes at school. They keep looking for him on the job because they are sure he will show up there, or they pay money to find him online because they know he just has to be there. Baby girl, you don't *know* where or when you will encounter that type of man you have envisioned in your heart. The fact is that he could come at a time and in a place that you least expect him. It is important, therefore, for you to live each moment with the recognition that this could be the time.

How would you dress and what would your hair look like if you knew that you were going to encounter him today? Remember, he has kingly potential, and he is looking for a woman with queenly potential. Would he recognize you as a princess? How would you behave if you knew the type of man you desire would be observing you? What if you're sitting in church gossiping about others, and he's sitting behind you listening to that conversation? What if he sees you ignore the instructions of an usher and push your way into a row where you insist on sitting? What if you are talking with a group of friends and it is your voice that he hears bellowing out above the others from twenty feet away? Would he think to himself, "That must be my queen I hear," or would he glance over with a look of disgust to see who is being so loud and rude? Your expectation determines your disposition. If you truly expected to meet your husband in any of those scenarios, you would dress, speak, and act accordingly. What is your expectation? Do you really expect to meet him?

Let's take that point to an even higher level. As you know, the parable in Matthew isn't about preparing for your husband on earth. It's about expecting Jesus to return. It's about the Parousia, the Second Coming. I truly believe all that the Bible tells us about Jesus. I believe that He died on the cross and God raised Him from the dead. I believe that He ascended into heaven and sits at the right hand of the Father, making intercession for me. And I believe that Jesus is going to come back someday in the same way He left, and He will be gathering His bride, the church, to Himself at that time. Now, because I believe that, my expectation impacts how I think, what I say, how I dress, what I do, and where I go. When Jesus comes back, I want Him to find me prepared and waiting for Him.

In the same way, if you truly believe that your husband is coming and today might be the day, your expectation will determine the way you live. Some women have lost that expectation, so they are living only for the moment. They are sleeping with other men, getting those men's names tattooed on their bodies, and developing a negative disposition because they have given up their hopes and dreams. They no longer even get any pleasure from their sexual encounters because they are meaningless. They hardly feel human anymore. They feel dirty, used, and disgusted with themselves, with men, and with life in general. Expectations are important.

You Can't Hurry Love

You could, of course, be asking about your man, "If he's coming, then what's taking him so long? I'm no kid anymore. I've waited all through high school, college, and a lot of years since, and he still hasn't shown up. If he really is coming, why is he taking so long to get here?"

Some people ask that same question about Jesus' return. What is taking Jesus so long to come back? There are a number of reasons. One of them, which serves as an analogy for us regarding the topic we're discussing, is based on His statement in John 14:2: He is going ahead of us to prepare a place for us. Once it is prepared, then He will come back to get us. One of the reasons Jesus hasn't returned yet is that He is not only preparing a place for us in heaven, but He is also preparing us for that place. If He came for us prematurely, the place might not be ready for us, or we might not be ready for that place. We have to trust God that His timing will be perfect and when it happens, we will all understand that, yes, it was the ideal moment. On this side of heaven, it seems at times that the delay is too long; but from heaven's perspective, which embraces all eternity, everything is right on schedule.

One of the reasons you and your husband haven't met yet is because God isn't through working with you. God is preparing you to be a queen. Remember that God wants the best for you. God wants you to marry a responsible Christian man—a man whose life has meaning and purpose, a man who knows how to love his wife, a man who has a father's heart and will love your children, a man who is ready for a "till death do us part" commitment. There are ways that God is still working with you so that you will be a Proverbs 31 woman for your kingly husband.

When all things are ready, you will connect. Daughter, don't get in such a hurry that you miss out because you are tired of waiting.

Once all that's straight, you will connect with a good man; but you don't know the day, and you don't know the hour. You don't want to get in such a hurry that you miss out because you say, "I'm tired of waiting; I'm going to do this by myself." I know you can get tired of waiting. Both the wise and the foolish virgins got tired and went to sleep. Why? Because it's normal and natural to get tired when something is taking so long to show up. But I would rather you wait on what is right than to rush into something wrong. Daughter, I would rather for you to patiently wait for a good man, the man who fulfills what you are looking for in a husband, than for you to rush into something with a lesser man and miss out on what God has for you.

It is important not to rush into marriage because over fifty percent of marriages today end in divorce, and most of them end within the first four years of the marriage. That's really sad. I don't believe the answer to a bad marriage is divorce. I believe the answer to a bad marriage is meeting needs. People go where their needs are being met. People like to be where they are being satisfied. A bad marriage can turn around if a wife seeks to meet her husband's needs and the husband seeks to meet his wife's needs. Tragically, too many men and women are too stubborn, self-centered, or proud to set aside their anger and pain to think about what their spouse needs. Meeting the other person's needs could change the whole situation, but they won't even try. So they endure four years of misery, four years of screaming and hollering, and four years of arguing before they finally say, "We can't take this anymore!" and seek a divorce.

Instead of rushing into a marriage unprepared, what if they had allowed God to use those four years to better prepare each of them for marriage? Rather than enduring four years of misery, anger, pain and yelling, they could have spent those four years seeking God to become a better Christian, a better man, a better woman, and a better person. The Supremes sang, "can't hurry love/No, you just have to wait/…love don't come easy/It's a game of give and take/You can't hurry love/No, you just have to wait/…trust, give it time/No matter how long it takes." Give yourself time, baby girl, to be prepared for marriage.

GOD MAY HAVE SOMETHING BETTER

Whenever I go to preach in Miami, Florida, I rent a car because I'm not just going to church. I know I'm also going to South Beach—one of my favorite places in all the world. One day I rented a car at the Miami airport and drove to the hotel. Because I was planning to have lunch in South Beach, I told the valet not to bother to park it in the garage because I would be back down in just a few minutes. I checked into the hotel, went to my room, and freshened up. A little while later, I called downstairs and told them I was coming back down for my car. They said, "Yes, Mr. Johnson, we'll bring it right away." I rushed back down, eager to get to South Beach for a nice lunch before preaching that night. In spite of what I had told them when I pulled in, they had parked the car in the garage anyway. Standing at the entrance of the hotel, I waited and waited. Finally, the valet came not with the car, but with the keys.

"Mr. Johnson, we've got a problem with your car."

"You didn't have a problem when I drove it in a short while ago."

"Well, your car has a flat tire."

"It didn't have a flat when I gave it to you less than an hour ago."

"It has a flat now. How do you want us to deal with this, Mr. Johnson?"

"I don't want you to deal with it. I want you to give me my keys. I know how to change a tire."

In my mind, I was thinking, "I'm going to change that flat in five minutes. I'll be eating lunch in South Beach in ten minutes. Then I can come back and rest before I preach tonight." So I went to the car and saw that they were right. The tire was flat. But I wasn't sweating it because I can change a flat in no time. I got into the trunk, took out the spare, took out the jack, and got started. I jacked up the car, took off the flat tire, and started to put the spare on, but the spare didn't fit. Of course, I was saying to myself, "Why would they rent me a car with a spare that doesn't even fit? Don't even put it in there if it doesn't fit . . . ." I was angry. Even though I had a beautiful car, it was all jacked up and I couldn't get to my destination. I called Hertz Rent-a-Car and said, "I've got a car that is jacked up because the tire is flat, and I can't put on the spare because it doesn't even fit. Why would you give me a spare tire that doesn't fit?" They responded, "Mr. Johnson, we are so sorry. If you will be patient with us, we're going to send somebody right out to deal with that situation."

I waited about an hour and a half. I tried to wait patiently, but it was hard because there was somewhere that I wanted to be. Yet there really wasn't anything I could do about it. I just had to wait. Now, I was expecting them to come out and fix the flat. But they didn't. An hour and a half later, they pulled up in a brand new candy-red Ford Mustang convertible with a black drop-top. They said, "Sir, we are so sorry for your inconvenience. Will you please give us the keys to the old car?" With great relief, I said, "Man, take this jacked-up situation and give me my new keys. Thank you very much!" Then I jumped into the new car, dropped the top, and headed to my destination.

Baby girl, don't get all worked up over a relationship that goes flat. Stop crying because it's all jacked up and isn't working. If you listen, you may hear God say, "I'm not going to fix that bad relationship. It isn't meeting your needs. It doesn't fit you. I've got something better in store for you. Just be patient, wait, and watch to see what I'm going to do." A delay isn't a denial. When you look at our Matthew 25 story, you read in verse 5: "The bridegroom was a long time in coming, and they all became drowsy and fell asleep." Just because the bridegroom delayed, it didn't mean he wasn't coming. He just didn't come as quickly as the bride and her bridesmaids anticipated. Note, too, that they didn't give up waiting for him. They didn't say, "Oh, let's just go. He isn't coming." They simply fell asleep; they didn't give up hope.

Don't Give Way to Temptation

We've already talked about how the foolish virgins ran out of oil before the bridegroom came, and tried to get the wise virgins to give up some of their oil. The wise ones said, in essence, "No, we're saving our oil for when the bridegroom comes." The foolish ones wanted them to give it up before the bridegroom showed up. The enemy will do the same thing with you, Daughter. The enemy will make you think that you need to give it up before your husband comes. But this parable lets us know that it's not giving it up that gets you the one you want. It was the *foolish* virgins who tried to get the wise virgins to give up their oil. They had already used theirs up. They were burnt out and empty and they had nothing left to give a husband. Then they tried to get the others to give theirs up. Don't listen when the enemy tries to get you to do something that you know isn't right.

Even those closest to God are tempted. Elijah encountered a situation like that. First Kings 19 tells us the story. Elijah had served God faithfully. He was obedient to do all that God told him to do. As a loyal prophet he shared God's message with the people and confronted false prophets. But one day he was under a great threat by an irate ruler. Elijah "ran for his life," verse 3 says. He ended up in a wilderness—tired, hungry, and alone. Verse 4 says, "He came to a broom bush, sat down under it and prayed that he might die." "I have had enough, LORD," he said. "Take my life; I am no better than my ancestors." Why was Elijah so depressed and suicidal? He reveals the reason later on, in verse 10 when he says to God, "I have been very zealous for the LORD God Almighty. The Israelites have rejected your covenant, torn down your altars, and put your prophets to death with the sword. I am the only one left, and now they are trying to kill me too."

Elijah was feeling bad because he thought he was the only one still serving God. He believed that everyone else had either been killed or had turned away from God and he alone was God's faithful servant. God didn't sympathize with Elijah's complaint. He told him to go back the way he came and essentially said, "You aren't the only one serving me. I've got seven thousand others in Israel who are doing My will. They didn't bow down to Baal." It was a trick of the enemy to get Elijah to think that he was the only one following God, the only one having a rough time, the only one suffering because he was waiting on God. Baby, the enemy will try that same tactic on you. Don't listen. Don't get discouraged. Don't give up. The bridegroom is coming.

When the Bridegroom Comes

The Matthew 25 parable tells us that the bridegroom finally does arrive and he, his bride, and their friends go into the wedding banquet. The marriage at last takes place. All of the bride's waiting is over. Her groom was delayed, but now he has finally come. Baby girl, when you and your husband come together, you must recognize that the waiting is now over. You refused to give yourself to others who were unwilling to give you a ring. You didn't let sex become a cheap thrill for you with other men along the way. You didn't give your body to other men even when they pursued you relentlessly. You've been waiting all this time, but now *the waiting is over*. Now is the time to let go.

There should be no holding back with your husband. Learn to enjoy expressing your love to him sexually. You don't have to do the same thing every time. You can experiment; you can have fun getting to know each other's bodies. Learn what makes him feel good, and let him know what makes you feel good. Don't bore your husband to death with reruns night after night. Present some blockbuster premieres from time to time. Think of how creative God is. You have been created in His image. Use your creativity in the bedroom, not only in decorating the living room. Remember that your husband has been waiting for you as well. Don't go to bed in your faded flannel nightgown every night and leave him asking God, "Is *this* what I was waiting for all that time?"

When the bridegroom came in our story, the bride and her bridesmaids went out to meet him. This appears to be symbolic of the fact that marriage is a "coming out" in some ways. It is a coming out of previous relationships, a coming out of grudges, a coming out of unforgiveness, and a coming out of projection. You can't let past experiences spoil this fresh new life that the two of you have together. If you are holding grudges and harboring unforgiveness in your heart against previous men who have hurt you, you need to let that go. Marriage has room for only one man and one woman. If either of you try to drag a former partner into your marriage, it will be too crowded and the marriage won't survive. You have to let go of the past in order to embrace the present.

You must be careful, too, that you do not project onto your new husband the behavior of your last man. Just because that last man broke your heart, you can't put a wall around your heart to try to protect it. Your husband is not that other man. Give him a break! Don't expect him to behave the same way as the man with whom you were in a relationship previously. And don't expect him to walk out because your father walked out on you and your mother. He loves you. He put a ring on your finger. He said, "Till death do us part." Get to know him without seeing him through your memory of another man. He won't be perfect, but baby girl, neither will you. Grow with him and learn with him how to nurture your marriage.

Marriage is not only a coming out, but also a going in. The bride and groom *go in* to the marriage relationship. You and your groom will be going in to the highest level of relationship that you will ever experience. As the wife, you are going into a place of submission. Ephesians 5 offers instructions to wives and husbands. Verse 22 says, "Wives, submit yourselves to your own husbands as you do to the Lord." If you aren't ready for that, don't go into marriage. Verse 33 says that "the wife must respect her husband." Remember, Daughter, that if you treat him like a king, you become a queen. Don't worry about becoming a doormat in this relationship. While you are respecting your husband and submitting to him, he is loving you even as Christ loves the church and sacrificed Himself for her (v. 25). It isn't hard to submit to a man who is laying down his life for you and caring for your needs even as he does his own.

MAKE YOUR HOME A HAVEN

Remember that you and your groom are entering a relationship that God has anointed and blessed. It is a special relationship. Notice that the door was shut to the foolish virgins. Even when they came knocking after getting more oil, they were not allowed in. Any wise woman knows that once she and her husband are together in marriage, she must lock out all foolish women. You don't need to allow any foolish women to offer you advice or give you counsel. You don't need to hear them talk about what they would do if he were their husband. You don't need to listen to that foolish mindset. Remember, they are foolish. Don't invite them into your home or your life.

While the foolish ones were locked out, the bride and groom went in. There was a marriage feast. Marriage is about joy and celebration, not about fussing and fighting or arguing and falling out. It's supposed to be about love, joy, peace, and harmony. You can help to make your marriage and home that way. You already know that your husband needs sex. You are now the only one who can satisfy this basic need that he has. See that you do it well. Your husband will also need some peace and quiet. He can't handle nagging or constant chatter. Twice in Proverbs it says, "Better to live on a corner of the roof than share a house with a quarrelsome wife" (Proverbs 21:9; 25:24). Dr. Oz says that a man who has to deal with a nagging wife is going to have his life cut short by eight years because of the stress. Make your home a place where your husband can hardly wait to come. When he thinks of you and your home, let him be filled with so much joy and love that his heart smiles throughout the day.

Remember, I told you earlier that the relationship between a husband and wife is symbolic of the relationship between Christ and the church. Jesus is the Bridegroom; the church is the bride. Every day, you should let Him know how much you love Him, how much He means to you, and how overjoyed you are that He is in your life. You know, too, that Jesus is coming again, even though you don't know the day or the hour. Being married to Jesus means a coming out: coming out of sin, out of unrighteousness, and out of this world's system and way of thinking. Being married to Jesus is also a going in. We go into Christ, even as Christ comes into us and makes us new creatures. We also look forward to one day going into heaven to a place he has prepared for us. Being married to Jesus is also about a locked door. We lock out the foolishness of the world that clamors for our attention and allegiance. And being married to Jesus is about joy and celebration.

Your Story Isn't Over

I sense, Daughter, that you may be thinking now not of the future and all that you have to look forward to, but of your past and all that you've missed. You know that you have already messed up in so many ways. You've already missed opportunities. You don't have any oil left, and you are no longer burning brightly. Your situation seems all jacked up, and you don't see any help on the horizon. You may be thinking of a good man who was once in your life, but now he's gone and you're thinking, "I missed it. It's too late for me." But let me assure you that it is not too late for you. Even if one man is gone, has remarried, has two children with his current wife, and your name never comes up, it's still not too late for you. Remember, I told you that it isn't about finding just one man, but rather one *type* of man. Christianity is about second chances. Even if we have messed up, our story isn't over. God gives us another chance, and God can still make something beautiful happen in our lives.

Lady Sharon and I were flying back from Jacksonville, Florida. We had a connecting flight through Atlanta, but there was a storm in Jacksonville, so we had to wait until the storm passed. We were delayed for so long that we realized we were going to miss our connecting flight in Atlanta that would bring us to our final destination in Indiana. So, we were on that plane to Atlanta, and I was frustrated and miserable because I was tired and didn't want to miss our connecting flight home. I looked at my watch and realized that the flight had already gone. We had missed our current connection because of what had transpired in the past.

While we were still flying at thirty thousand feet, I told Sharon, "When this plane lands, we are going to *run* to the service counter because we want to be the first ones there to get on the next flight." "Sharon," I told her, "there are more people on this plane who want to get on that next flight than they will have room to accommodate. So, we are going to outrun them. As soon as we get off this plane, we're going to take off running, find that service counter, and get them to reconnect us on the next flight because we've already missed our scheduled one." I was so intense about this. "Do you understand?" I asked her. She said, "Jeffrey, I know what you're saying." I said, "Okay." When the plane landed, I said, "Sharon, give me all of your stuff. Give me everything you've got so that you will be free to run faster." She said, "Okay."

We got off the plane and literally ran through the Atlanta airport. We were going at it. When we finally got to the service counter, there were no human beings, only electronic kiosks. Now, I'm technologically challenged. I needed a human being there to hear my story. I needed to explain that we had come out of a storm and that we had missed our flight. I wanted to say to that person, "You've got to connect us. And hurry up. I want to get two seats before everybody else comes." But there were no human beings to listen to my plight, so I had to learn real fast how to use technology at a kiosk. I figured it out. I took one of our boarding passes that we already had, slid that bar code under the light of the kiosk, and when I did that, out came a new boarding pass. It already had the next flight, the next time, and even our seat assignment. Rebooking us had happened automatically before we even got to this airport. Before we even made the request, we were already automatically rebooked. The airline thought so much of us that when they realized we had just come out of a storm, which caused our flight to be delayed, and we had missed our connection, they had already taken care of us.

Now, if an airline thinks that much of us, don't you think Almighty God thinks even more of us? You don't need to run and rush about like a crazy person. You don't need to try to brush past everyone else and leave them in the dust so that you can be first. God knows you've been through some storms. He knows there have been some delays. Baby, all you need to do is show up where you need to show up because the Holy Spirit has already automatically rebooked you. That last man is gone, but God has another one on the way! He loves you that much!

Epilogue

DIALOGUE WITH MY FATHER

Thank You, Father, for giving me
all I need for my journey on earth.
Thank You for Your mercy and grace
You have showered upon me from my birth.
Thank You for allowing and arranging in my life
situations that strengthen me.
Thank You, Father, for love, truth, and joy—
inspiration for all I can be.

You taught me that I am so much more than my hair,
far more than just how I look.
I'm Your daughter with a heart, mind, and soul like Yours
—a child of God whose name's in Your book.
I am a spiritual being created in Your image
and designed for Your own good pleasure.
I am so very wonderfully and fearfully made,
and my specialness should be treasured.

You taught me, my Father, to handle my body
which is a temple that belongs to You.
I am to be Christlike and not like the world
in all I say, think, and do.
I'm to respect my body and take care of it,
for it is where Your Spirit lies.
And I am to keep my cookies in the cookie jar
until You say otherwise.

You taught me, Father, to handle my brain:
to free my mind and the rest will follow.
You want me to think like a child of God
and to look to You as my Model.
I'm to study Your Word so I may know You better,
expressing Your likeness accordingly.
My choices will determine my consequences;
my mentality will determine my destiny.

You taught me, Father, to handle my business:
to get my money straight.
Who I am, what I become, does not depend
upon any man to validate.
For You have given me confirmation and identity;
I will flourish when I plant, plan, and praise.
I will prosper when I produce and not merely consume,
and trust in You always.

You taught me to handle my blessings:
to "do me" just as You intended.
I am Your child, which makes me royalty;
my kinship will never be rescinded.

I am blessed beyond riches with all You provide;
with the world's wealth, I am not impressed.
For You are the King, my Ultimate Joy,
who always gives me what's best.

Who gives this woman? You'll someday hear asked
as my prince waits to give me that ring.
In him, You'll see a man after Your own heart
and You'll know that our love's the real thing.
On our wedding day, when that question's asked
and my earthly dad answers, "I do,"
I pray, Father, that You will smile proudly at us,
and say, "My daughter, I do, too."

Thank You, Father, for our dialogue;
I recognized Your voice.
Your words enlightened and inspired me
to always make the best choice.
I thank You for Your blessings and kindness, O Lord;
Without You, there would be no me.
But Father, above all that I'm grateful for,
I thank You for just being "Daddy."

by Jan Abdul Rahim